FIELD GUIDE TO

BACKYARD BIRDS OF THE MID-ATLANTIC

Published by Cool Springs Press
A Waynick Book Group Company
101 Forrest Crossing Boulevard
Suite 100
Franklin, Tennessee 37064
(615) 277–5555

ISBN-13: 978-1-59186-010-5

First Printing 2008
Printed in the United States of America
10 9 8 7 6 5 4 3 2 1

Project Manager: Ashley Hubert
Art Director: Marc Pewitt
Production: Publication Services, Inc.
Illustrator: Publication Services, Inc.

Photographs of the American Tree Sparrow and American Woodcock courtesy of Jupiter Images. All other photographs provided by Brian E. Small.

FIELD GUIDE TO

BACKYARD BIRDS OF THE
MID-ATLANTIC

COOL
SPRINGS
PRESS

FRANKLIN, TENNESSEE

CONTENTS

INTRODUCTION

The Mid-Atlantic region is dominated by two geographic features: the wind-battered coasts of the Eastern Seaboard and the rugged Appalachian Mountains. The oak-hickory forests covering these gentle slopes are home to the brilliant cerulean warbler, while the pine-oak woodlands along the coast are alive with dark-eyed juncos, tufted titmice, and American redstarts.

Although numerous species breed in the Mid-Atlantic states, the most exciting seasons for bird watching are spring and autumn, when large flocks of blackbirds, warblers, and other species pass through backyards in droves on their way to northern breeding ranges. Along the coast, transient birds such as the American golden plover can be spotted as they make the epic 10,000-mile journey between northern Canada and South America. Whatever the season, this region hosts an array of diverse bird species sure to keep even experienced birders on the lookout.

If you are new to birding, a few basic strategies will increase the likelihood of spotting and identifying local species. The first step is to obtain at least one useful field guide. Carry it with you in the field, and keep it on hand for easy use. When you sight an unfamiliar bird, watch its behavior, note its coloring and unique field marks, and then consult your guide to confirm its name.

The second item to keep handy near your observation window is a pair of binoculars. A quality pair can often be purchased for under $100, and 7x or 8x magnification is ideal.

Learning to recognize bird songs is another valuable investment. Audio CDs and online resources provide samples of hundreds of common bird calls and songs, and knowing the sounds of your common backyard residents will make it easier to recognize an uncommon visitor.

Consider joining a local birding club. These organizations frequently organize birding walks and field trips, where more experienced birders can answer your questions, help you identify unfamiliar species, and recommend the best local bird-watching sites.

The simplest way to begin birding is to watch the birds in your own backyard. Even a small yard with one or two feeders can be home to dozens of birds. Some affordable options for seed-eaters include black-oil sunflower seeds, white millet, peanuts, mixed seed, cracked corn, and thistle seed. Insectivores may be happily

Cerulean Warbler

at home among garden trees and shrubbery, but in winter, many turn to berries and suet cakes. Still others—hummingbirds, for example—are drawn to flowering plants.

Learning the dietary preferences of your favorite species can help you decide how best to draw them to your property. Bird boxes for cavity-nesting species are another easy way to intimately observe their behavior. Whether you encounter feathered friends close to home or far afield, birding is sure to become an exciting and rewarding hobby.

red

nesting sites and food in cities, towns, and farming areas.

Feeding Habits

Finches are common visitors to backyard seed feeding stations, and otherwise survive on fruit, bread crumbs, berries, buds, and flower parts.

Migration Habits

The introduced eastern population has thrived and spread across the continent, now separated from the native western population by less than 100 miles.

Placement of Feeders

While these welcome visitors are perched on your mixed seed feeder, try to distinguish the female house finch from the female house sparrow. Also, watch for finch nests in your hanging flower baskets or ornamental garden trees.

In 1940 New York City pet shops began to sell California's native house finches as pet songbirds. In the ensuing crackdown on this practice, a small population of the brightly plumed birds was released. Eventually spread to suburban communities throughout the East.

Description

Similar to the purple finch of the North and West, the 6-inch male is brown above with a red brow, bib, and rump. The female, identified by a white eyebrow, and juvenile are paler with streaked bellies.

Preferred Habitat

Now widespread and common in both the East and the West, the house finch competes with the house sparrow for

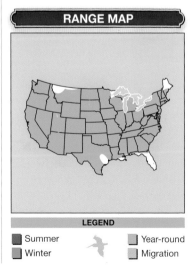

RANGE MAP

LEGEND

■ Summer	■ Year-round
■ Winter	■ Migration

Northern Cardinal

Unusual among birds, cardinals mate for life and stay paired year-round. The colorful pair sings in duets, completing each other's loud whistled phrases *what cheer, cheer, cheer* or *sweet-sweet-sweet-sweet*. The male may act aggressively toward the female at a feeding station, but she continues feeding, undisturbed.

Description
Named for the robes of Catholic cardinals, the male's bright red plumage and black face are unmistakable. Females are grayish brown with red highlights on the crest, wings, and tail, and an orange-red bill. Both measure 7.5–9 inches long.

Preferred Habitat
Common in gardens, parks, thickets, woodlands, and hedgerows, cardinals nest in a shrub or a tangle of vines.

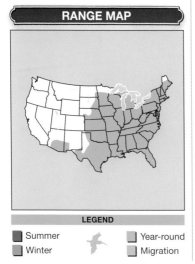

RANGE MAP

LEGEND
- Summer
- Winter
- Year-round
- Migration

Males feed the first brood while the female starts a second, with up to four broods each year.

Feeding Habits
Cardinals have a varied diet encompassing weed seeds, wild fruit, insects, grains, and even maple syrup from woodpecker holes.

Migration Habits
These nonmigrants are less territorial in winter, joining with small flocks. In recent decades their range has extended farther north.

Placement of Feeders
This frequent feeder visitor uses its short, conical bill to crack open seeds, especially sunflower seeds, safflower seeds, and cracked corn.

Purple Finch

red

During spring migration, from late March to early May, the colorful male finch, giving sharp *chip* calls in flight, is a common and welcome sight.

Description
Though similar to house finches and Cassin's finches, purple finches are the most uniformly red. Males, 5.5–6.5 inches long, are red above and below, fading to a pale stomach. The sparrow-like female is brown, heavily streaked below, with whitish markings on her face.

Preferred Habitat
These finches usually nest in conifers, but that may include ornamental conifers in gardens or parks. They are also found in mixed and coniferous woodlands and bottomland forests.

Feeding Habits
Finches thrive on box elder, ash, and sycamore seeds, as well as maple, birch, and aspen buds. Fruit and berries provide sustenance in winter, and insects are a treat in summer.

Migration Habits
Generally these birds breed across most of Canada, but can also be found year-round along the Pacific Coast. But when food in the northern forests is scarce, purple finches flood their southern range.

Placement of Feeders
Year after year, small groups of purple finches return to their favorite feeders, especially those featuring sunflower seeds, where these birds lend a splash of color and a rich, cheery song to the winter landscape.

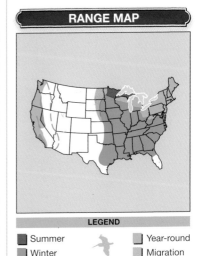

RANGE MAP

LEGEND

■ Summer ■ Year-round
■ Winter ■ Migration

A bristly layer of feathers protects the nostrils from wood dust as the woodpecker hammers out a rapid message on a utility pole. This sturdy bird is equipped for a lifetime of climbing and drilling, bracing itself upright with a stiff tail and using its long toes to grip its perch.

red

Description

The 10-inch woodpecker is stout and strong, ladder-barred black and white above with a tan face and underparts. Males have a characteristic red crown and nape, while females have a red nape only.

Preferred Habitat

Any orchard, park, farmland, or open swampy woodland with a handful of dead trees might be home to the red-bellied, which bores a nest hole in dead tree trunks or utility poles.

Feeding Habits

Its stiff bill chips away bark to find insects, wood-boring beetles, seeds, and wild fruits. Its long, cylindrical tongue has a hard tip to spear insects and a sticky coating to lap up ants.

Migration Habits

Found in the East, northernmost birds may migrate south in winter, where they are common in parks and southeastern woodlands.

Placement of Feeders

Listen for the woodpecker's low, hoarse rattling call. In winter they turn to feeders, and those wintering in Florida suck juice from oranges.

RANGE MAP

LEGEND

- ■ Summer
- ■ Winter
- ■ Year-round
- ■ Migration

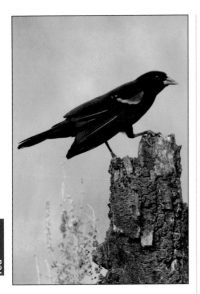

Ｆrom his perch on a swaying cattail, the male blackbird sings his gurgled song while flashing his red shoulder patches, eagerly establishing his mating territory before the females arrive.

Description

This large blackbird, 7–9.5 inches, is common and unmistakable. The black male has bright red patches on the shoulders, bordered by a yellow band. Females and juveniles are heavily streaked with brown and lack the red patches.

Preferred Habitat

Perhaps most common in marshes, swamps, and wet meadows, this marsh bird will nest near any body of water, including dry pastures, farmland, and roadside ditches. Breeding birds construct a new nest of marsh reeds for each of the season's two or three broods.

Feeding Habits

Seeds provide the blackbird's main sustenance in spring and autumn, but it switches to insects for the summer season.

Migration Habits

Their extensive breeding range stretches across the United States, and the birds winter north to Washington, Michigan, and Pennsylvania.

Placement of Feeders

The flashy red-wing is a familiar sight in backyards and parks across the country, particularly when they join up with other blackbirds for autumn and winter feeding in mobs of hundreds of thousands or even millions.

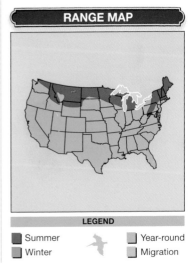

RANGE MAP

LEGEND

- ■ Summer
- ■ Winter
- ■ Year-round
- ■ Migration

With wings vibrating 50–60 times per second, fast enough to produce a humming noise, the beloved hummingbird is the only bird that can fly backwards or hover like an insect. The ruby-throated is the only hummingbird found east of the Mississippi.

Description

At only 3.5 inches, this tiny bird is stunning metallic green above and white below. Adult males have a bright, iridescent red throat, but females have a white throat and breast, buff sides, and white outer tail feathers.

Preferred Habitat

These nectar-feeders follow the flowers, and they are common residents of suburban gardens, parks, and woodlands. During courtship, males

perform a pendulum-like dance for the calm females, buzzing with each dip.

Feeding Habits

A thin, needle-like bill gets nectar from tubular red flowers such as petunia, salvia, bee balm, and trumpet creeper.

Migration Habits

Despite their small size, hummingbirds travel extraordinary distances, breeding from southern central Canada to the Gulf Coast and wintering in Mexico and Central America.

Placement of Feeders

Their frenetic motion makes hummingbirds tough to spot in the field, but a garden featuring the bird's preferred flowers or red tube nectar feeders can attract them.

RANGE MAP

LEGEND

- Summer
- Winter
- Year-round
- Migration

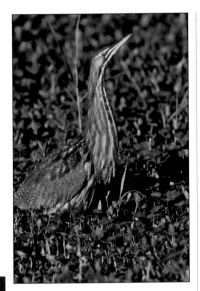

grassy lakeshores, large wetlands, or wet meadows.

Feeding Habits
Standing in the shallow water, the bittern waits in perfect stillness until a hapless fish draws near, then it plunges its stiff beak into the water to stab its meal.

Migration Habits
This water-loving bird breeds throughout the northern half of the United States but can be found year-round along the Pacific Northwest coastline.

Placement of Feeders
In March and April, the usually solitary, silent males make brief public courtship displays. Between dusk and midnight, listen for a low-pitched *oonk-a-lunk* call.

brown

This master of disguise is so well camouflaged that birders may walk right past without noticing him. Sitting silently with its bill turned straight up to the sky, the bittern can take on the appearance of a tree stump, a root, or a dead limb, or it can sway back and forth to blend in perfectly with its reedy home.

Description
The pear-shaped bittern ranges from 24–34 inches long, streaked dark brown above, with dark wingtips and yellow legs and feet. Its white throat has long, reddish brown stripes.

Preferred Habitat
In secretive, isolated pairs the bitterns build a reed platform nest near the water's edge in marshes, fens,

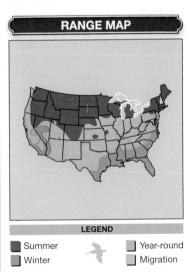

RANGE MAP

LEGEND

■ Summer   ■ Year-round
□ Winter   □ Migration

This small bird, only 10 inches long, makes an incredible journey each spring and autumn of nearly 10,000 miles over the Atlantic between Canada and South America, or over the Pacific to Australia for its well-deserved winter rest.

Description
Spring adults are mottled black flecked with gold above and below, with a white S-shaped stripe from the crown to the shoulders. By autumn they molt into whitish underparts, with less gold above and a paler eyebrow.

Preferred Habitat
During spring migration the birds rest in agricultural fields on their way to their breeding grounds in the tundra of northern Canada and Alaska. During autumn migration they prefer mud flats and sod farms.

Feeding Habits
Plovers consume mainly insects, mollusks, and crustaceans, but often fatten up on crowberries before their long journey.

Migration Habits
Flocks of 500 to 5,000 pass through the central United States during spring migration from South America to the far North. In autumn, much smaller flocks cruise along the Atlantic Coast.

Placement of Feeders
Watch for tired birds riding the winds or resting in wet crop fields during migration periods. Plovers were once hunted in huge numbers, but they are now federally protected and their populations are bouncing back.

RANGE MAP

LEGEND

- Summer
- Winter
- Year-round
- Migration

brown

They relocate to marshes, wetlands, and swamps.

Feeding Habits

In 24 hours a woodcock can eat its weight in earthworms, plucking them out of the loose earth with its long bill. They also consume insects, berries, and the seeds of some grasses and weeds.

Migration Habits

This early migrant nests long before the spring's final frosts. They are found east of the Great Plains, breeding in the north and wintering in the southern half of their range.

Placement of Feeders

From mid-March to June, but especially in April, listen for the male's sensational courting song, or their common *peent* call.

brown

During spring courtship, the male woodcock gives a fascinating display. After sunset, and sometimes all night long, he parades around his territory buzzing like an insect, then leaps into flight crooning a warbling song, then dives in zigzags back to the ground.

Description

Stocky and large-headed, the 11.5-inch woodcock is mottled brown with a camouflage leaf pattern above and rust or buff below. The bill is very long, and the eyes are set far back beneath a black-barred crown.

Preferred Habitat

Woodcocks raise their broods in brushy fields, moist thickets, or damp woodlands. After breeding season,

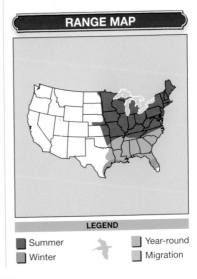

RANGE MAP

LEGEND

Summer   Year-round

Winter   Migration

I n the resounding darkness of the deep woods at night, a chilling call rings out—*Who cooks for-you, who cooks for you-all?* The nocturnal barred owl is a varied vocalist, with calls that include hoots, howls, barks, and squawks.

Description

At 18–24 inches, this squat owl is twice the size of the eastern screech-owl, and females are slightly larger. Its ruffled plumage is brown above and pale below, with dark horizontal barring across its chest, vertical streaks on the belly, and white barring down its back.

Preferred Habitat

In dense woodlands, river valleys, or swamps, females lay eggs on the bare floor of a tree cavity, in a simple wooden nest box, or in an abandoned hawk's nest.

brown

Feeding Habits

Although primarily nocturnal, the barred species is often seen hunting during daylight, seeking mice, frogs, snakes, insects, rodents, small owls or birds, and crayfish.

Migration Habits

Owls are common year-round in the East and along the Pacific Coast to California.

Placement of Feeders

On overcast afternoons, their unique calls can lead you straight to their roosts, where they are calm and tame. Also try imitating their simpler calls to lure them near.

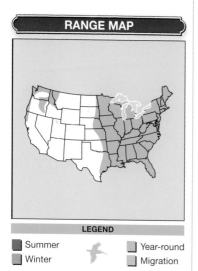

RANGE MAP

LEGEND

- Summer
- Winter
- Year-round
- Migration

Feeding Habits

To minimize competition with other warblers, this bird scours mid-level branches for caterpillars, spiders, flies, budworms, and insect larvae. In their wintering grounds in South America, they eat mostly fruit.

Migration Habits

In summer they are found in parts of Minnesota and New England. In winter they cross the continent on the way to Panama and Colombia.

Placement of Feeders

Watch for this common migrant from May to June, when they are easy to identify, but once they drop their breeding plumage, males look very similar to blackpoll warblers.

This warbler's population fluctuates in relation to cyclical infestations of spruce budworms, pests that devastate spruce forests. In infestation years, there may be up to six times as many bay-breasted warblers.

Description

Measuring 5–6 inches long, breeding males have chestnut on the crown, throat, and sides, with a black face and forehead, a pale ear patch and buff underparts. Females are similar but lack the side patches. Nonbreeding males are dull green with buff sides.

Preferred Habitat

In spruce forests across Canada, the bird builds a bulky cup of twigs, bark, and grass in a conifer. During budworm years, females lay two additional eggs.

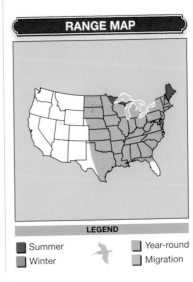

RANGE MAP

LEGEND

Summer

Winter

Year-round

Migration

Just before dawn, while a female songbird is away from her nest, an intruder rolls an egg out of the nest and replaces it with her own. The imposter fledgling will dominate the other chicks until it grows to maturity and rejoins its original species, the brown-headed cowbird. Often vilified as a brood parasite, the female cowbird leaves more than 20 eggs each season in the nests of more than 200 other species.

brown

Description

The 6–8 inch glossy black male has a brown head, while the female is grayish brown overall. Both issue a *check* or rattling call.

Preferred Habitat

Once found only in the Great Plains, where it followed roaming buffalo herds, the brown-headed cowbird has thrived on suburbanization and is today found from coast to coast, favoring woodland edges, thickets, roadsides, and towns.

Feeding Habits

Alongside other blackbirds and starlings, the cowbird forages on the ground for insects, seeds, and grains. Grasshoppers are a particular favorite.

Migration Habits

Migrating throughout the West in summer, these birds are found year-round in the Mid-Atlantic, Midwest, and along the entire West Coast.

Placement of Feeders

This bird is drawn to grains, seeds, berries, cracked corn, or sunflower hearts.

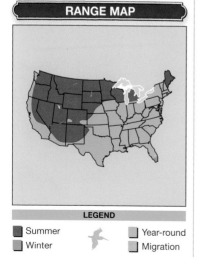

RANGE MAP

LEGEND

- Summer
- Winter
- Year-round
- Migration

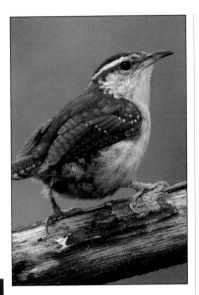

brown

Feeding Habits

Flitting from plant to plant, these omnivores eat primarily insects and other small animals, as well as fruit and seeds.

Migration Habits

Carolina wrens inhabit the Mid-Atlantic and Midwest year-round, never migrating, which means that a harsh winter can devastate populations. But young birds seem to expand northward after mild winters. They mate long term, staying paired year-round.

Placement of Feeders

As the only wren to frequent garden feeders, these cheery singers are drawn to fruit and suet, peanut butter, sunflower seeds, and nuts. They will often nest in birdhouses or other man-made objects, such as baskets, mailboxes, stone walls, or tin cans.

Switching without pause from *wheat-eater, wheat-eater, wheat!* to *tweedle, tweedle* or *tea kettle, tea kettle,* the Carolina wren sings up to 40 different songs all day long, regardless of season.

Description

Although similar to the house wren, the Carolina wren can be identified by its upturned tail. Measuring 6 inches, the bird is mainly reddish-brown with a white eyebrow swash, white chin, and buff underparts.

Preferred Habitat

Found in woodlands, thickets, undergrowth near water, and garden shrubs, the wren constructs small nests of grass, stems, and bark in a tree cavity or man-made object.

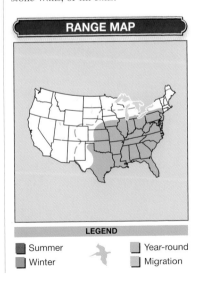

RANGE MAP

LEGEND

■ Summer ■ Year-round
■ Winter ■ Migration

Cedar Waxwing

These sleek, elegant birds are highly social, often seen lined up on a wire or branch passing berries or flower petals from one bird to the next. Best identified by a narrow, black "bandit" mask across the eyes, the crested bird has yellow tail tips and waxy red tips on the inner wing feathers.

Description

The 8-inch waxwing's plumage is a beautiful blend of soft pastel browns and grays above and below.

Preferred Habitat

Waxwings enjoy the close company of their own kind, making them one of the few songbirds to nest in colonies. They build bulky twig nests in open woodlands, orchards, gardens, and parks.

brown

Feeding Habits

The bird consumes mainly berries and flower buds from berry-bearing trees and shrubs, especially cedar cones. Overripe, fermenting berries cause temporary intoxication, a startling sight for observant birders. During summer they also catch insects.

Migration Habits

This stunning species breeds across the northern half of the United States wintering in the lower United States from the East Coast to the West Coast.

Placement of Feeders

Announcing their arrival with a high-pitched whistling, small winter flocks frequently descend on parks and gardens in search of cedar and rowan berries.

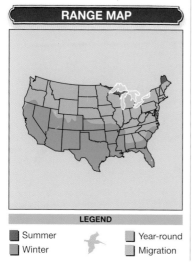

RANGE MAP

LEGEND

■ Summer
■ Winter
■ Year-round
■ Migration

Chimney Swift

brown

Long ago abandoning its traditional habitat, the chimney swift selected the hollow towers accompanying human settlements for its home, both in nesting season and during migration. At sundown swarms of these fast flyers funnel like a tornado into large chimneys.

Description
Shaped like a boomerang in flight, the 5.5-inch swift is one of the world's fastest flying birds. Adult birds are dark gray-brown all over, with a short, stubby tail and long, narrow, curved wings.

Preferred Habitat
This species is found in all habitats across the East. Adults use saliva to glue a twig nest onto a vertical wall within a chimney, barn, well, or tree cavity. A second male often assists with raising the fledglings.

Feeding Habits
The swift spends its life on the wing, swallowing insects whole as it flies and dipping into rivers and streams to drink and bathe.

Migration Habits
These birds breed from the Great Plains east to the coast, traveling to South America in September.

Placement of Feeders
Large flocks return to favorite chimney sites year after year. In place of suitable chimneys, specially designed towers can be erected to draw flocks to your own property.

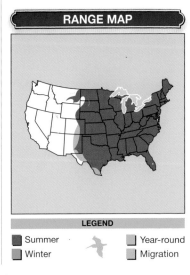

RANGE MAP

LEGEND

■ Summer   ■ Year-round
■ Winter   ■ Migration

Dunlin

Originally named "dunlings," meaning little dun-coloreds, these small, plump sandpipers measure only 6–8 inches.

Description
Breeding adults are reddish above and white below, with a large black patch on the belly. Winter adults are grayish brown above and whitish below. The best field mark is their long, black, downward-curving bill.

Preferred Habitat
The male reaches breeding grounds in Arctic or subalpine tundra in early June and awaits his devoted mate's arrival. Together they build a ground nest, sharing incubation and feeding the chicks. During migration and winter, dunlins can be found on mud flats, and on beaches along ponds, lakes, or oceans.

brown

RANGE MAP

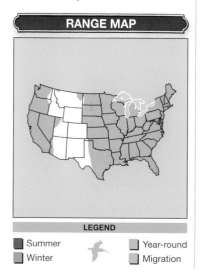

LEGEND
- ■ Summer
- □ Winter
- ■ Year-round
- ■ Migration

Feeding Habits
This species consumes small marine animals, crustaceans, mollusks, and insect larvae. They particularly favor marine worms, which minimizes competition with other shorebirds.

Migration Habits
Usually seen along the Pacific, Gulf, and Atlantic Coasts, these birds breed across northern Canada. If they migrate too early, finding the tundra marshes still frozen, they may head south for a few more weeks.

Placement of Feeders
In winter dunlins form large flocks of up to tens of thousands, but they do not mingle with other species. They are tame and can be approached quite easily.

Fox Sparrow

brown

During spring migration, the otherwise elusive fox sparrow conspicuously spouts loud, melodious warblings from a shrub or thicket. This sparrow—a separate genus from other sparrows—has 18 different subspecies in North America.

Description
Western birds are brownish or slate-colored and red-striped. Eastern birds are fox colored with orange-red wings and tail and blue-gray highlights on the head. The Rockies version is gray above with a reddish tail, while sparrows of the Pacific Northwest are darker above with a slightly reddish tail. All measure approximately 7.5 inches.

Preferred Habitat
As a ground nester, the sparrow makes its home in dense woodland thickets, overgrown coniferous forests, or in grassy pastures or roadsides.

Feeding Habits
Equipped with unusually large feet and claws, the fox sparrow, like the eastern towhee, finds its meals by noisily double scratching among leaves for seeds, berries, or insects.

Migration Habits
Though most of its breeding range is found throughout the Rocky Mountain range, this sparrow winters in the Mid-Atlantic and all along the West Coast.

Placement of Feeders
A smacking *tssk!* call or noisy scratching in leaves reveals the backyard presence of this shy visitor. Red cedars or elderberry bushes draw the sparrows in winter.

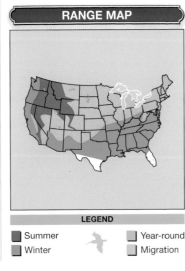

RANGE MAP

LEGEND

■ Summer ■ Year-round
■ Winter ■ Migration

Grasshopper Sparrow

Named for its insect-like song, a male grasshopper sparrow perches on a dried weed stalk singing *kip-kip-kip-zeee*, then flits off to chase a female, emitting sounds too high-pitched for human hearing. The clever female can make a display of injury to lure away predators, and conceals the location of the nest by walking to it through tall grass.

Description

This small grassland sparrow, measuring only 5 inches, is dark, scaly-patterned rust above, with a buff breast, pale stripe on crown, short pointed tail, and dark eyes.

Preferred Habitat

Grassland options vary by region, but the grasshopper sparrow prefers open, weedy meadows or pastures, including airports. These birds are sensitive to change, and their populations decline as overgrown fields are cleared for urban development.

Feeding Habits

Foraging among grass clumps, this bird eats seeds, spiders, grasshoppers, and other insects.

Migration Habits

The northern two-thirds of the United States (and, rarely, Florida) are breeding grounds for the bird, where they nest in loose colonies. When the weather turns, they winter across parts of the southern United States.

Placement of Feeders

If you have the option, mow or cultivate paddocks and hayfields late in summer to avoid destroying their ground-level nests.

RANGE MAP

LEGEND

■ Summer
■ Winter
■ Year-round
■ Migration

brown

Gray-cheeked Thrush

In a scraggly tree on the barren Arctic tundra, a male gray-cheek pipes its sweet, fluting song for up to 20 hours of daylight. Unfortunately for North American birders these birds are fairly quiet during migration and are heard less commonly than the Swainson's or Hermit thrushes.

Description

This 8-inch thrush is dull brown or olive-brown above and whitish below, with large dark spots on the breast and neck. The species is named for its gray cheek patch.

Preferred Habitat

In stark contrast to their South American rainforest wintering grounds, the birds breed in sub-Arctic woodlands and willow and alder thickets. Females construct a nest of mud and plants near or on the ground.

Feeding Habits

The ground-foraging thrush ingests mainly ants, but also spiders, earthworms, caterpillars, mollusks, beetles, and fruit.

Migration Habits

This bird's bi-annual journey of up to 8,000 miles is a greater distance than any other thrush travels. Like the Swainson's thrush, this nighttime migrant risks collisions with tall buildings and TV towers.

Placement of Feeders

In spring and autumn the gray-cheeked species is common and widespread, but easily overlooked as it spends most of its time quietly foraging on the ground.

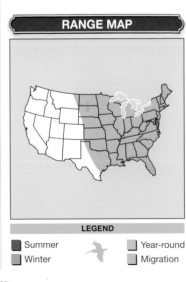

RANGE MAP

LEGEND

- Summer
- Winter
- Year-round
- Migration

Startled from the edge of a reedy pond, a compact, dark-colored bird utters a sharp *kowp* call and explodes into flight. This shy bird, formerly called the green-backed heron, avoids the open habitats of other herons and is less commonly sighted.

Description
Significantly smaller than other herons at 16–22 inches, the green heron has a dark head, gray-green or gray-blue back, chestnut cheeks and neck, and bright orange or yellow legs.

Preferred Habitat
Nesting in isolated pairs or small colonies, green herons are drawn to freshwater or brackish marshes, rivers, ponds, or streams with muddy banks and thick clumps of weeds or trees for cover.

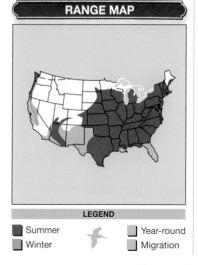

RANGE MAP

LEGEND

Summer

Winter

Year-round

Migration

Feeding Habits
Crouching, log-like, on the muddy bank, the patient hunter dangles a leaf from its bill to attract fish to the surface. Stretching its neck, the heron takes aim, flicks its tail nervously, and stabs an unsuspecting fish. Frogs, crustaceans, and insects are also prey for the diminutive heron.

Migration Habits
Though rarely seen, the heron is widespread east of the Rockies and along coastal California, southern Arizona, and Texas. Small flocks head south in winter.

Placement of Feeders
Approach carefully and quietly to spot the green heron hunting at the edge of a water source.

brown

Hermit Thrush

A lovely, hymn-like fluting song at twilight has earned the hermit thrush much admiration. Its long, rolling notes vary in pitch and volume, making it difficult to pinpoint the songster.

Description
The 7.5-inch thrush is olive-brown above and boldly spotted buff below. The face is gray with a white eye ring, but the best field mark is its reddish tail.

Preferred Habitat
This forest bird can be found in coniferous or deciduous woodlands or wooded swamps, bogs, and fields. The female builds a well-concealed ground nest, and the male helpfully feeds his incubating mate.

Feeding Habits
In spring and summer the bird forages on the ground and gleans vegetation for ants, butterflies, bees, moths, and spiders. In winter they subsist on wild fruits, buds, and berries.

Migration Habits
If you spot a spotted thrush in winter, it must be the hermit thrush. This species winters across the southern United States, but as soon as beetles emerge in early spring, they head north into the Rocky Mountain range and along the Pacific Northwest Coast.

Placement of Feeders
Suet cakes, raw apples, pecans, and peanut butter may attract this woodland bird to a backyard feeder. Watch for its characteristic tail-bobbing; this is the only thrush to wag its tail.

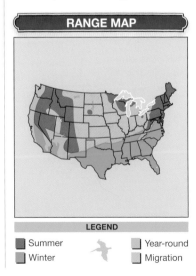

RANGE MAP

LEGEND
- Summer
- Winter
- Year-round
- Migration

Of the world's 75 true lark species, the horned lark is the only one widespread in North America. The clearing of eastern forests made way for this bird of open spaces, which often makes its home on prairies, air fields, farmland, or Arctic tundra.

Description

Although its black "horns" are rarely visible, the 8-inch lark is very distinct with its black markings on the head and black crescent band across the breast. The face is white or yellow and the black tail is rimmed with white.

Preferred Habitat

In a spectacular courtship display, males soar to heights of up to 800 feet, then nose-dive silently back down. Their nests—in a shallow depression on the bare ground—are vulnerable to late storms or spring planting.

Feeding Habits

Walking slowly along the ground and scratching with its large feet, the horned lark searches for grain, seeds, insects, or spiders.

Migration Habits

This bird breeds all across the United States except in the Southeast; its yearly migration takes it to the West Coast.

Placement of Feeders

Larks gather in flocks of up to thousands in late autumn, often joining with longspurs and buntings. They may be seen along roadsides or croplands, often singing in flight.

brown

RANGE MAP

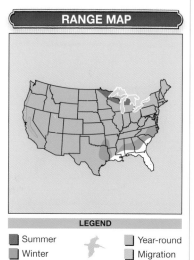

LEGEND

■ Summer
■ Winter
■ Year-round
■ Migration

In an effort to control crop pests, house sparrows were imported from England in 1850 and released all over the United States. They have since spread throughout the entire continent, where they thrive in human-altered environments (part of their Latin name is *domesticus*). Unfortunately, these aggressive competitors have diminished the success of native cavity nesters such as bluebirds and tree swallows.

Description

Males, up to 6.5 inches long, have a gray crown and rump, black bib, white cheeks, and chestnut head stripes, while the female and young are streaky brown above and white below.

Preferred Habitat

Resourceful and friendly, the house sparrow is at home in cities, suburbs, and farmland, where it constructs nests of grass, feathers, and bits of rubbish in a man-made or natural cavity.

Feeding Habits

The sparrow squabbles fiercely over territory, mates, and food, the latter including insects, grains, berries, and weed seeds.

Migration Habits

Some birds of the past experienced involuntary migration, touring the country by rail while snacking on spilled grain in train cars, but the house sparrow has become an abundant permanent resident throughout North America.

Placement of Feeders

A familiar sight at every backyard feeder, house sparrows are drawn to bread crumbs, seeds, and grain.

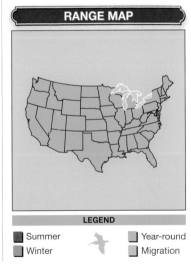

RANGE MAP

LEGEND

Summer ⬛ Year-round ⬛
Winter ⬛ Migration ⬛

Nearly every vacant lot or golf course is home to this noisy plover. When threatened, the adult bird feigns injury, dragging its wing as if broken, to lure predators away from the nest. These shorebirds flee by sprinting along the ground or swimming to safety.

Description

Named for its shrill *kill-deer* alarm call, the species measures 9–11 inches, colored brown above and white below, with a rust-colored rump, long legs, and a black-and-white tipped tail. Adults have two identifying black bands across the chest, though chicks have only one.

Preferred Habitat

Any short-grassed open field, river bank, or gravel road edge with water nearby can house the killdeer, where

brown

it nests in a shallow depression in the ground.

Feeding Habits

Like other plovers, killdeers feed with a stop-start action of chasing prey and standing still, then pecking in the dirt with their bills to seek seeds and insects, earthworms, and snails.

Migration Habits

As early as February, some killdeers migrate north to breed. However, they can be found from the East Coast to the West Coast throughout the year.

Placement of Feeders

Killdeers are common and easy to identify, but if you spot an adult male giving the broken-wing display, retreat and do not disturb them.

RANGE MAP

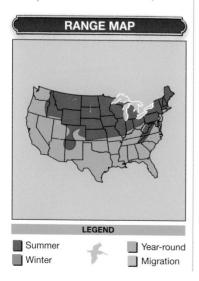

LEGEND

- ■ Summer
- ■ Winter
- ■ Year-round
- ■ Migration

brown

reeds. These plants are used to construct a nest attached to reeds.

Feeding Habits
This flycatcher consumes aphids, beetles, wasps, bees, mites, and larval dragonflies, and plucks other aquatic insects and snails from their marshy home.

Migration Habits
This bird has an extensive breeding range spanning the United States from north to south. It can be found year-round, however, only along the Atlantic and Gulf Coasts and in the far West.

Placement of Feeders
Patient observation in the bird's habitat may be rewarded with a brief glimpse of its cocked tail. Listen for the male's call, reminiscent of a mechanical sewing machine.

The polygamous male builds up to 20 "dummy" nests to serve as courting sites for potential mates. Interested females then construct their own nests. This abundance of nests, most unused, makes it difficult for competing species to enact revenge when the marsh wren pierces the eggs of nearby wrens and larger blackbirds.

Description
Smaller than a sparrow at 4–5.5 inches, the wren is brown above, pale buff below, with a white-streaked back and white eyebrow. Males define and defend their territory with up to 200 different songs.

Preferred Habitat
The marsh wren prefers wetlands, particularly freshwater or brackish marshes with abundant cattails, bullrushes, or

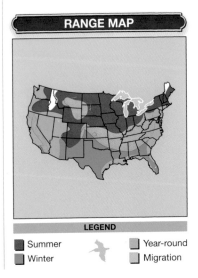

RANGE MAP

LEGEND

Summer — Year-round
Winter — Migration

With 70 million shot annually, the mourning dove ranks as America's most popular game bird. The species boomed with the large-scale felling of forests, and its mournful *coo-ah, coo, coo* song is recognizable in all urban and suburban environments.

Description

This 12-inch sandy-colored dove has black wing spots and a long tapered tail bordered with white. Males are slightly brighter, with a pink sheen along the neck.

Preferred Habitat

The resilient mourning dove thrives from farmland to irrigated deserts, open fields, parks, and lawns. Their stick nests, built in tall trees, low bushes, or on the ground, are flimsy and poorly constructed, but home to at least two broods annually.

brown

RANGE MAP

LEGEND

■ Summer
■ Winter
■ Year-round
■ Migration

Feeding Habits

Like other doves and pigeons, this dove feeds its young regurgitated, protein-rich food known as "pigeon milk" produced in the adult's gullet. Birds may fly several miles at dawn or dusk in search of seeds, insects, or the nearest water source.

Migration Habits

Hundreds of birds may congregate for autumn migration from the southwest regions of Canada south throughout the continental United States.

Placement of Feeders

The backyard birder has only to listen for the dove's song to recognize this frequent feeder visitor. Watch for their fast, smooth silhouettes flying at early morning or dusk.

Northern Flicker

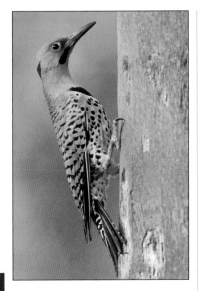

A loud, repeated *flicker* or *wick-wick-wick* ringing in the forest canopy announces the breeding season of this unusual woodpecker. Three color variations exist—yellow-shafted (East), red-shafted (West), and gilded (Southwest)—but they interbreed where their ranges overlap.

Description

Large at 10–14 inches, flickers are black or brown with tan bars above, with a pale spotted breast and bright underwings. Eastern birds have yellow under the wings, a red nape, and a black "mustache" on males. Western birds have red underwings, rump, and mustache. Southwestern varieties have yellow underwings and a red mustache.

Preferred Habitat

Spot the flicker in open country near large trees, such as farmlands, parks, woodlands, deserts, and suburbs. They nest in a tree cavity or burrow into fence posts, rafters, or even saguaro cacti.

Feeding Habits

Foraging on the ground, the flicker extends its enormous tongue to lap up ants. It also consumes insects, fruit, and seeds, occasionally flycatching.

Migration Habits

Although year-round residents of the United States, these birds migrate north for the breeding season and return south to winter in south Texas and in the Desert Southwest.

Placement of Feeders

Watch for these ground feeders eating ants and beetles on lawns or sidewalks. They may also visit suet feeders.

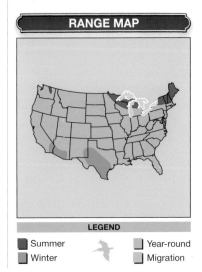

RANGE MAP

LEGEND

Summer
Winter
Year-round
Migration

From spring breeding season through autumn, and even into winter in the North, the aptly named song sparrow serenades his mate with more than 20 different songs, improvising more than 1,000 variations on these melodies.

Description

Coloring varies from rust to gray to streaked brown above, but all measure 5-7 inches long, with a brown eyebrow and a central spot in a streaked white breast. Juveniles lack the central breast spot and may be mistaken for the savannah sparrow.

Preferred Habitat

Song sparrows make their homes in thickets, gardens, parks, and roadsides, where they raise up to three broods each year. Fledglings begin to develop their own song repertoire

before they even leave the nest.

Feeding Habits

These ground feeders use their feet to rustle up insects, seeds, grain, and berries. In flight, watch the sparrow's characteristic pumping of its long, rounded tail.

Migration Habits

Traveling solo or in pairs, song sparrows are found throughout the United States year-round, but winter from the Deep South into the Desert Southwest.

Placement of Feeders

Although common and widespread in North America, a song sparrow at a backyard feeder is a rare occasion. But if you locate a nearby nesting pair, watch for them to return year after year.

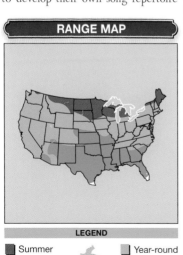

RANGE MAP

LEGEND

■ Summer ■ Year-round
■ Winter ■ Migration

brown

Feeding Habits

The talented thrush has several foraging strategies to maintain a varied diet. From the ground it gleans ants, beetles, bees, wasps, and crickets, but it can also hover high in treetops to snatch insects from foliage. In autumn and winter it consumes cherries, grapes, and elderberries.

Migration Habits

Early spring marks the thrush's long migration from the tropics to its breeding grounds from Alaska to northern New England, and south in the mountains to southern California, Colorado, and West Virginia. An evening traveler, Swainson's thrush often fatally collides with tall buildings and TV towers.

Placement of Feeders

Listen for a plunking *whoit* call from the clear evening sky in spring or autumn.

Named after nineteenth century English naturalist William Swainson, this ground-dwelling bird is very similar to the hermit thrush. Its increasing, spirally song, though arguably less beautiful than that of the hermit thrush, is better known because the bird sings constantly during migration.

Description

Once known as the olive-backed thrush, the 7.5-inch bird is solid olive-brown above and spotted below, with a buff eye ring and cheeks.

Preferred Habitat

In a small forest shrub or tree the thrush conceals a lichen-decorated moss nest. They are common residents of coniferous forests, mixed woodland, and willow thickets.

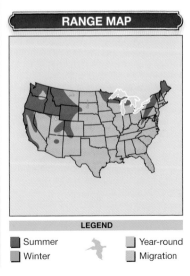

RANGE MAP

LEGEND

Summer   Year-round
Winter   Migration

Once known as the bay-winged bunting, this familiar farmland sparrow was renamed for its sweet serenade to the setting sun. This ground dweller alights on the highest available perch to sing its descending trill throughout the day, but it is the only sparrow to sing regularly at twilight.

Description

The 6.5-inch vesper sparrow is streaked gray-brown above and pale and streaked below. Its white-rimmed tail and orange-red shoulder patches are the best identifying field marks.

Preferred Habitat

This bird is one of only a handful of species common in prairies, fields, meadows, and roadsides in farm country. The nest is sunk into a shallow dent in the ground, leaving their broods vulnerable to the threat of early mowing or cultivation.

Feeding Habits

Running along the ground, the vesper sparrow halts to pick up grain, weed seeds, and insects. Its fondness for agricultural pests, such as weevils make it a welcome addition to cultivated fields.

Migration Habits

The coastal states, from California to New England, are wintering grounds for these songsters, but breeding season is spent across the north half of the United States, with the great numbers of them in the West.

Placement of Feeders

Scatter cracked corn below your feeding stations to draw solo birds or mating pairs in winter and early spring.

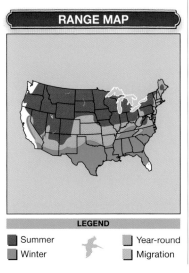

RANGE MAP

LEGEND

■ Summer
■ Winter
■ Year-round
■ Migration

two broods. Nests are frequently parasitized by brown-headed cowbirds.

Feeding Habits
The thrush's springtime diet consists almost entirely of insects, such as beetles, ants, and butterflies, but by late summer it eats mainly plants, berries, and seeds.

Migration Habits
In late April flocks migrate from Central America to the Great Plains and east to the Atlantic.

Placement of Feeders
This is the only thrush to regularly nest near human dwellings, but they seldom visit feeding stations. They are welcome residents in gardens because they eat cutworms and beetles.

P raised by American author Henry David Thoreau as the most beautiful song of any bird, the male wood thrush sings his sweet, liquid melody *ee-o-lay, ee-o-lay* at dawn and again at dusk, sometimes joined by the female's equally lovely song from the nest.

Description
At up to 8.5 inches, the starling-sized wood thrush is the largest bird of its family in the East. Adults are olive-brown above and dark-spotted white below. The bird's face is streaked black and white, and its crown is reddish.

Preferred Habitat
In damp mature forests, parks, and gardens with large shade trees, the mating pair combines mud, grasses, and moss to craft a sturdy nest for the season's

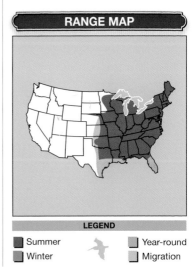

RANGE MAP

LEGEND
Summer	Year-round
Winter	Migration

brown

This finch is commonly known as the wild canary for its appearance and song. As it hops along summer fields gleaning thistle seeds, the male bird's bright yellow and black plumage is unmistakable.

Description
The summer breeding male is easily recognized, with its lemon-yellow coloring, and black cap, wings, and tail. At 5 inches long, the female and winter male are significantly duller yellow with black wings and tail.

Preferred Habitat
Fields, groves, thickets, farmland, and weedy grasslands provide a steady supply of small insects and seeds year-round.

Feeding Habits
In spring, when insects are plentiful, they account for up to 50% of the goldfinch's diet. Seeds are its main staple through late summer and autumn, with berries supplementing in winter.

Migration Habits
Spring is ideal breeding time in western states, but in the East goldfinches commonly wait until late summer, when weed seeds are readily available. They travel in flocks of up to 20, but are hardy enough to winter across much of their normal range.

Placement of Feeders
Feeders offering nigel thistle seeds and sunflower seeds are sure to draw these birds to your yard, and they are frequent visitors during the winter months. The goldfinch also loves birdbaths.

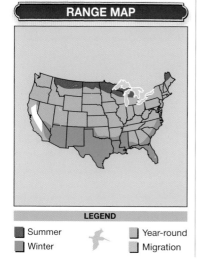

RANGE MAP

LEGEND
Summer

Winter

Year-round

Migration

yellow

Blackburnian Warbler

Scientists recently discovered that although this warbler is similar to four other warblers that may share a common food source and even perch in the same conifer, each species uses different foraging techniques and lives at a different level from the ground.

Description
The spring male is streaked with black and white, with a bright yellow throat, eyebrow, and crown patch. The female is similar but more yellow and grayish, with two identifying brace marks on her back. The 5-inch creature issues thin, fast, high-pitched calls *sleet-sleet-sleet* and *tiddly-tiddly-tiddly*.

Preferred Habitat
Coniferous forests, as well as oak-hickory woodlands in southeastern mountain ranges, provide high perches for these foragers.

Feeding Habits
Like several other warblers, the Blackburnian warbler dines on insects and berries.

Migration Habits
Your best chance of spotting these otherwise elusive birds is from the last week of April through mid-May, as they migrate toward Canada and the Northeast in large flocks.

Placement of Feeders
These shy critters are best identified by their call and then sought among the high treetops, where they may appear at the ends of branches searching for bugs among the foliage.

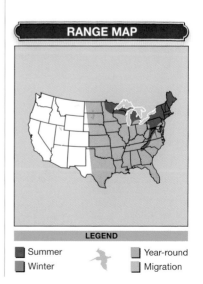

RANGE MAP

LEGEND

■ Summer   ■ Year-round
■ Winter   ■ Migration

Until 1997, this bird was classified as a solitary vireo, but is now distinguished as a distinct species. The attractively colored blue-headed vireo is a fairly common migrant, seen earlier in the spring than other vireos. It is extremely tame and not threatened by human presence.

Description
Olive green above and white below with yellow flanks, the 6-inch vireo features a slate blue head with bold white spectacle markings.

Preferred Habitat
The blue-headed species is the only vireo to inhabit coniferous forests, where it nests in the forked twigs of small trees.

Feeding Habits
Like other vireos (and distinct from

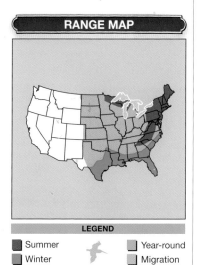

RANGE MAP

LEGEND

■ Summer ■ Year-round
■ Winter   ■ Migration

wrens), these slow fliers scan the trees for insects, hovering to pluck caterpillars, wasps, moths, butterflies, stink bugs, beetles, ants, spiders, or bees. Berries of dogwood trees may also catch this deliberate feeder's interest.

Migration Habits
Unique among vireos for their solo migrations, these birds are found in the eastern half of the United States, wintering in South Carolina and southward along the Gulf Coast.

Placement of Feeders
Friendly and fearless, these curious birds are comfortable on human territory. Listen for their slow, slurred calls. They have even been known to sit quietly and allow their feathers to be stroked.

Common Yellowthroat

Often called the Maryland yellowthroat, where it was first collected in 1766, this sweet songbird is elusive and rarely seen. The male yellowthroat twitters from perch to perch, marking his territory and defending it aggressively.

Description
The small black-masked male issues a sharp *chek* call from his bright yellow throat. The 6-inch female, lacking the mask, responds with a gentle *wichity, wichity* song.

Preferred Habitat
Brushy swamps, wet thickets, or overgrown marshes, and tangles of weeds or berry bushes provide sufficient cover for the ground nests of these polygamous birds.

Feeding Habits
Hovering low over a clump of cattails, the yellowthroat scoops up adult and larval insects such as spiders or dragonflies, supplementing its diet with seeds.

Migration Habits
Migrating from South and Central American into the entire United States during summer, this species is the northernmost yellowthroat in the western hemisphere. Though not its usual habitat, the migrating birds may be found far from water.

Placement of Feeders
This shy but curious species can be roused from their tall-grass hideouts by various noises. Try making a squeaking noise by kissing the back of your thumb, give a low growl, or make a *psssh-psssh* sound.

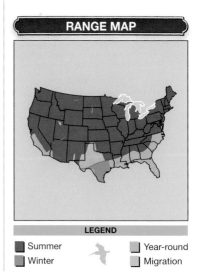

RANGE MAP

LEGEND

■ Summer   ■ Year-round
□ Winter   ■ Migration

Although actually in the blackbird family, the meadowlark is so named for its singing ability. The eastern and western meadowlarks are identical in appearance, habitat, and feeding and nesting habits, but have vastly different songs. A clear, high-pitched, wistful trill of *see seer seee-u* sets the eastern meadowlark apart from its western counterpart's longer, confident, gurgling song.

Description
Streaked black and brown on top and measuring 8–10.5 inches, this species has an eye-catching lemon yellow and black breast. The western species is paler and grayer.

Preferred Habitat
Weaving blades of prairie grass to make a dome, the female meadowlark constructs her ground nests in grasslands, pastures, and marshes. If the nest is destroyed by mowing, these polygamous breeders will nest again.

Feeding Habits
Grain and seeds round out a diet comprised mostly of insects, including spiders, beetles, grasshoppers, crickets, caterpillars, weevils, ants, and wasps.

Migration Habits
Traveling in groups, bright meadowlarks can be found in almost any grassy, open area. They occupy the eastern United States year-round, migrating slightly northward in summer.

Placement of Feeders
Look for these shy feeders perched on fence posts. They may be drawn to seeds and grain spread on the ground.

RANGE MAP

LEGEND

■ Summer
■ Winter
■ Year-round
■ Migration

yellow

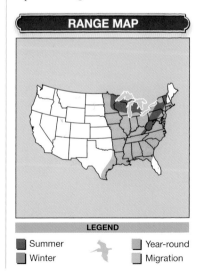

species resides in overgrown fields and briar-rich pastures, abandoning fields when they become heavily forested.

Feeding Habits
The acrobatic warbler swings upside down to pick caterpillars and insects from the underside of foliage or hovers to snatch insects from leaves.

Migration Habits
Arriving in May, the warbler's short breeding season begins. By July, the fledglings leave the nest and the flocks return to South and Central America for the winter.

Placement of Feeders
If caterpillars are plentiful in your area, watch this colorful warbler consume mass quantities during April or September migration.

This bird is closely related to the blue-winged warbler, and these species interbreed where their ranges overlap, producing fertile hybrid offspring called Brewster's warblers; these offspring, in turn, produce Lawrence's warblers. The hybrid birds have coloring similar to either parent species, but with yellower bellies.

Description
Resembling a chickadee, the 4.5 inch male is gray above, white below, with a black mask and throat, yellow crown and wing patch, and white spots underneath the tail. The female has a gray mask and throat.

Preferred Habitat
Generally preferring drier areas than the blue-winged warbler, this ground-nesting

RANGE MAP

LEGEND
- Summer
- Winter
- Year-round
- Migration

yellow

The loud, clear whistling song of this colorful warbler makes them a welcome guest during spring and autumn migrations. Among wood warblers and within their own species, each bird has a specified habitat and feeding area or strategy, allowing peaceful coexistence with minimal competition.

Description

The handsome male, 5.5 inches long, is olive above and yellow below, with a yellow face and black hood and throat, while the duller female lacks the hood. Both have white tail spots that flash as they bound from branch to branch.

Preferred Habitat

In mature, mixed forests, especially ravines or wooded swamps, the warbler makes its home no more than 10 feet above the ground. Females produce two broods annually, as their low-lying nests are often predated by snakes.

Feeding Habits

Males catch flying insects and glean insect larvae from leaves and shrubs, while females hunt insects and spiders close to the ground.

Migration Habits

During their winters in the tropics, males and females select separate habitats, and only males return to the same mating grounds each year.

Placement of Feeders

Although not a likely visitor to suburban gardens, the hooded warbler is easiest to see during spring migration, in early to mid-April.

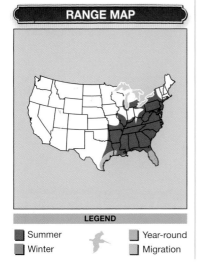

RANGE MAP

LEGEND

- Summer
- Winter
- Year-round
- Migration

Kentucky Warbler

yellow

This shy bird spends the majority of its time foraging and skulking within dense shrubs or thickets, making it tough for all but the most persistent birder to spot.

Description

Olive above and bright yellow below, the 6-inch bird is best identified by its yellow spectacle markings and black forehead, crown, and cheek. Females have a gray crown and paler cheeks.

Preferred Habitat

Deciduous forest with ferns, briars, or other dense undergrowth is the ideal home for this warbler. The female incubates alone in a grassy nest on or near the ground, but the male abandons his soliloquies to help feed the chicks when they hatch.

Feeding Habits

This species has more diverse foraging methods than its relatives, alternately hopping along the ground, plucking caterpillars and spiders from foliage in the forest canopy, or chasing insects in flight.

Migration Habits

The bird was discovered in 1811 in Kentucky, but is no more common in that state than in the rest of its range. It summers in the East, migrating to the Yucatan Peninsula in September for winter.

Placement of Feeders

Listen for the male's rich, persistent *turdle, tur-dle* song during spring courtship. Unmated males often continue to sing throughout the summer.

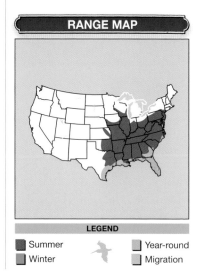

RANGE MAP

LEGEND

■ Summer ■ Year-round
□ Winter □ Migration

The mourning warbler's scientific species name *philadelphia* denotes where it was first discovered in 1810, though it is a relatively rare migrant through that city. Its common name can be credited to the male's dark hood and black chest patch that resemble mourning dress.

Description

Measuring 5.5 inches, these handsome olive warblers are bright yellow below with a gray hood. Males have a black patch on the chest, while females have a gray throat. Their counterpart in the West, MacGillivray's warbler, is identical except for its white eye streaks.

Preferred Habitat

Dense briar and berry thickets or other heavy undergrowth in damp forests provide the mourning warbler's preferred cover for its ground nest. Occasionally it breeds in coniferous forests as well.

Feeding Habits

Caterpillars, spiders, beetles, and other insects found in dense shrubbery form the basis of the bird's diet.

Migration Habits

In spring these warblers migrate from their tropical winter home across the continental United States to reach their breeding grounds in the North.

Placement of Feeders

From within dense foliage a loud *check* call or *cheery-cheery-chory-chory* song gives away the presence of this chipper backyard visitor as he hunts for insects.

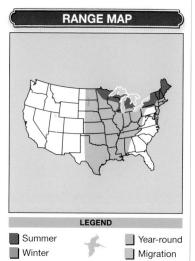

RANGE MAP

LEGEND

■ Summer
■ Winter
■ Year-round
■ Migration

yellow

young woodlands, and groves. Its ground nest is securely hidden under a sapling or shrub, or in a clump of moss.

Feeding Habits

This insectivore scours leaves and flowering plants for spiders, beetles, aphids, caterpillars, flies, and grasshoppers.

Migration Habits

Highly localized populations breed throughout California north to Washington and from Minnesota across New England. Most winter in Mexico, but small groups remain along the coasts of California and Texas.

Placement of Feeders

Watch for this iridescent warbler during spring migration. Its two-part song is a high-pitched *see-it, see-it, see-it* followed by *ti-ti-ti-ti*.

In 1811, when Alexander Wilson discovered this warbler in Tennessee, the bird was not a common resident. But the clearing of vast forests generated the overgrown pasture favored by the Nashville warbler, now a common migrant throughout much of North America.

Description

This 5-inch warbler is olive above and bright yellow below, with a white patch on the belly between the legs. The male's pearly gray head has a white eye ring and a usually concealed red crown patch. Females have an olive-colored head and a blue-gray neck.

Preferred Habitat

During migration the warbler can be found in woodlands, shrubs, and suburbs, while it breeds in brushy fields,

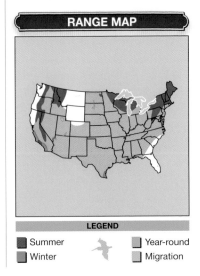

RANGE MAP

LEGEND

■ Summer	■ Year-round
■ Winter	■ Migration

L ike the American tree sparrow, this bird is not found in the habitat its name would suggest. This small songbird prefers second-growth forests that spring up following logging or burning.

Description

Tiny at 4 inches, the warbler is olive-green above and yellow below, with two white bars on dark wings and a dark eye stripe. Males have rusty stripes down the back, and females have olive rather than black stripes on the face.

Preferred Habitat

This warbler prefers young stands of pine, deciduous saplings, or mangroves. The nest is a cup of plant down in a low tree or shrub. Like some other warblers, females commonly eat the eggshells (a source of calcium) after their young hatch.

Feeding Habits

This insectivore occasionally catches flying insects on the wing, but generally gleans grasshoppers and spiders from foliage.

Migration Habits

In early spring the prairie warbler leaves its home in the Caribbean and heads north to breed in the East and South, from Texas to Maine.

Placement of Feeders

No other olive-backed yellow warbler shares this bird's habit of "wagging" its tail while perched. Listen for both versions of the male's rapid, buzzy song, one to court females and the other to warn away competitors.

yellow

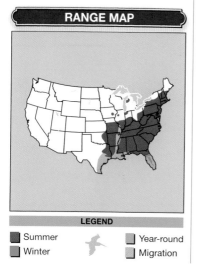

RANGE MAP

LEGEND

■ Summer   ■ Year-round

■ Winter   ■ Migration

yellow

Darting about along the tallest tree-tops, small energetic birds scoop up insects from the tips of branches while singing a staccato song ending in a loud trill.

Description
Summer breeding males, at 4–5 inches long, are olive green above, whitish below, with a gray crown and a thin line across each eye. Winter males are olive above and yellowish below, and females are similar but duller.

Preferred Habitat
Tennessee warblers construct their nests in clumps of grass or sphagnum moss at the base of a shrub in open, mixed forests or wooded swamps.

Feeding Habits
On their first journey south, fledglings forage quietly in low vines and shrubs, but by the trip in the following spring, the flocks forage high in the forest canopy for insects, spiders, berries, and seeds.

Migration Habits
From its wintering habitat in South America these warblers cross the majority of the United States on their long journey to Canada, but their main migration route is along the Mississippi Valley. Their breeding range overlaps with northern Wisconsin and Maine.

Placement of Feeders
Watch for these flighty warblers in May during their spring migration, but note that populations vary significantly from year to year.

RANGE MAP

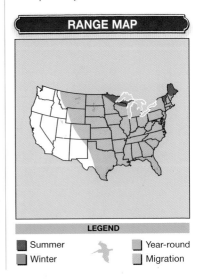

LEGEND

■ Summer   ■ Year-round
■ Winter   ■ Migration

This usually silent bird has a tendency to sing at the approach of a storm, earning it the nickname "rain crow." Its unique call is a rapid, rattling *ka-ka-ka-kow-kowp-kowp-kowp*.

Description

Slender and long-tailed, the bird measures 10–12.5 inches, colored brown above and white below with a yellow and black bill. In flight, note the large white spots under the tail and the red patches on the wings.

Preferred Habitat

The cuckoo crafts a flimsy twig nest in a bush or a small sapling in orchards, damp thickets, overgrown fields, or suburban parks. Although not classified as a nest parasite, the cuckoo will sometimes lay eggs in its black-billed relative's nest or those of other birds.

Feeding Habits

A taste for hairy caterpillars and tent worms makes this bird useful for keeping agricultural pests in check. Their varied diet also includes fruit and berries, small bird eggs, and tiny amphibians.

Migration Habits

In spring the cuckoos travel from their South American wintering grounds to parts of California, along the Rockies, north to Minnesota and east to the coast.

Placement of Feeders

Even backyard cuckoo residents are shy and easily overlooked, as they rarely draw attention to themselves. Watch for them in late summer during temporary swarms of cicadas.

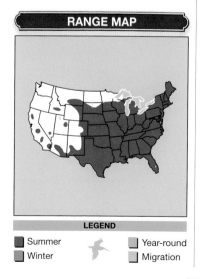

RANGE MAP

LEGEND

- Summer
- Winter
- Year-round
- Migration

yellow

F ormerly the yellow-rump was thought to be two species, the eastern myrtle warbler and the western Audubon's warbler. The breeding males of each region look distinct, but they interbreed freely.

yellow

Description

Breeding males, 5–6 inches long, are dull blue above streaked with black, with a black breast and flanks and bright yellow on the rump, crown, and sides. Eastern males have a white throat and two white wing bars, whereas western males have a yellow throat and a large white wing patch. Females and juveniles always have the yellow rump.

Preferred Habitat

For summer breeding these warblers prefer coniferous and mixed forests, forest edges, and overgrown and cultivated fields, where they build bulky twig nests in conifers. During other seasons they forage in a variety of habitats.

Feeding Habits

Winter populations are heavily dependent on poison ivy berries, while summer birds consume insects and berries.

Migration Habits

The widespread warbler breeds from the Pacific Northwest to New England and south to Mexico in the western half of the country. Winter finds them roosting in pine forests from their breeding range to the tropics.

Placement of Feeders

In winter these birds frequent gardens but rarely visit feeders. Listen for their frequent *chip* call to distinguish them.

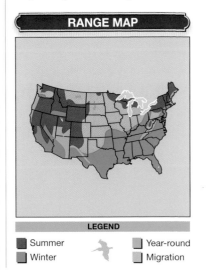

RANGE MAP

LEGEND

■ Summer
■ Winter
■ Year-round
■ Migration

Males of the species are easily identified, looking just as their name describes in both breeding and nonbreeding seasons. Unlike most warblers, the females look so unlike the males that early naturalists thought they were different species.

Description

Males are blue-gray above and on the crown, with a black face, bill, throat, and sides. Females are olive above and dark buff below with a small white patch on the wings. Both measure up to 5.5 inches long.

Preferred Habitat

Within a dense rhododendron or a mountain laurel, the mating pair constructs a nest near the ground with twigs, grass, ferns, and leaves. During migration, they are found in mixed forests

with plenty of deciduous saplings.

Feeding Habits

Primarily an insectivore, the black-throated blue warbler gleans or fly-catches for caterpillars, spiders, moths, or other insects, but also consumes berries and seeds as available seasonally.

Migration Habits

This colorful warbler is found in the United States only in summer, from Wisconsin in a wide swath eastward to New England and south to Florida.

Placement of Feeders

If American yew or the bird's preferred nesting shrubs are planted on your property you'll be able to observe these tame birds at close range.

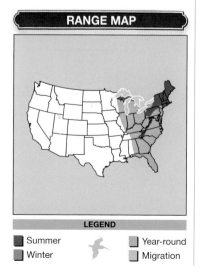

RANGE MAP

LEGEND

- Summer
- Winter
- Year-round
- Migration

blue

These brightly colored, noisy birds have a mixed reputation. Both tame and curious, they warn other birds of danger and mob predators. Yet they also eat fledglings of other species and can imitate a hawk's screech or other bird calls to claim feeders for themselves.

Description

At 12.5 inches, this large bird has an unmistakable bright blue crest, back, wings, and tail, with white tail tips, face, and underparts. Issuing a repertoire of boisterous calls, its own soft *queedle-queedle* song is seldom heard.

Preferred Habitat

Jays inhabit forests of all kinds, but oak forests are preferred. They are also common residents of gardens and parks.

Feeding Habits

One of the few birds to cache food, the jay buries seeds and acorns for winter, indirectly planting new trees. Nuts, seeds, fruits, insects, mice, and bird fledglings comprise its diet.

Migration Habits

Traveling in flocks, these birds can be found from the eastern slopes of the Great Rocky Mountains to the Atlantic Coast. Its counterpart west of the Rockies is Steller's Jay.

Placement of Feeders

These backyard bullies are frequent feeder visitors in winter, and they love sunflower seeds, suet, cracked corn, and peanuts. They are comfortable around humans, but may mob birds, squirrels, cats, or even great horned owls.

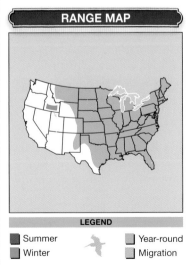

RANGE MAP

LEGEND

Summer — Year-round
Winter — Migration

The incessantly active gnatcatcher cocks and flicks its long tail as it bounds through the branches. These tiny birds are fearless, readily attacking crows, jays, or other large predators who threaten their territory.

Description

Measuring 4–5.5 inches, the gnatcatcher is blue-gray above and white below with a long, black tail edged with white. Breeding males have an identifying black eyebrow, but in winter their gray eyebrow matches the female's.

Preferred Habitat

In summer the bird is at home in open mixed woodlands, especially juniper groves. Its tiny lichen-decorated nest hooked to thin twigs is often parasitized by brown-headed cowbirds. As mating pairs take turns incubating the

eggs or feeding the fledglings, the male warbles incessantly at top volume.

Feeding Habits

This quick flyer can pursue fleeing insects through the treetops, hover to pick insects and spiders from leaves or flowers, or snatch tiny gnats from the air. In autumn they join mixed foraging flocks.

Migration Habits

Breeding throughout most of the United States gnatcatchers winter in select regions, one being the Desert Southwest.

Placement of Feeders

Track down this hyperactive bird by following its nasal *meehr* or buzzy *spee* call. Their high-pitched song will lead you right to their nest.

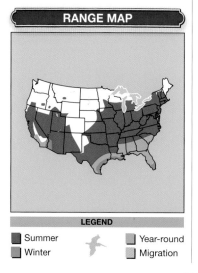

RANGE MAP

LEGEND

- Summer
- Winter
- Year-round
- Migration

blue

Cerulean Warbler

Although notoriously tough for bird-watchers to identify with any certainty because they live high in the forest canopy, try listening for series of quick, accelerating buzzing sounds and a higher buzzing drone to indicate the presence of these warblers. They may soon be added to the threatened species list as populations have reduced drastically in much of their range.

Description

Aptly named for its coloring, the 5-inch adult male is light blue above and white below, with a dark breast band. The female and juvenile look similar but are often tinged with green, lacking streaks or the breast band.

Preferred Habitat

Rich deciduous and mixed forests are the habitat of choice for this warbler. Females construct nests on long branches of box elder trees, where their coloring provides good camouflage.

Feeding Habits

In the highest levels of the forest, these shy birds rummage in foliage for insects such as caterpillars.

Migration Habits

Unlike most birds, the cerulean warbler has a discontinuous range, breeding in loose colonies across the Mid-Atlantic and Midwest and wintering in the tropics.

Placement of Feeders

The cerulean species is difficult to distinguish from other warblers, but with careful observation it can be sighted singing in treetops from dawn to dusk.

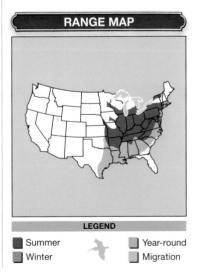

RANGE MAP

LEGEND

| Summer | Year-round |
| Winter | Migration |

In forests east of the Rockies, a gentle bird whispers a sweet *tru-al-ly* song from its perch in a pine. Although once widespread, the eastern bluebird has been crowded out of nesting sites by starlings and house sparrows. Its regeneration depends largely on man-made bluebird houses.

Description

The male, 5-7 inches long, is bright blue above, with a rusty orange throat and white belly. The paler female has a brown-ringed back and rusty throat.

Preferred Habitat

In summer, look for them near pines, orchards, open woodlands, or on mountain slopes. Forming family groups in winter, they roost in grassland or farmland.

Feeding Habits

From a low perch, the bluebird swoops to snatch up insects, particularly spiders and grasshoppers, which comprise 80% of its diet. Berries provide extra sustenance in winter months.

Migration Habits

Inhabiting the southern half of its breeding range year-round, populations may be threatened by long freezes. They nest in woodpecker holes, birdhouses, or other safe cavities, where the young of the season's first brood help raise the second.

Placement of Feeders

Monitor your bluebird houses to prevent habitation by aggressive starlings. The easily tamed bluebirds love birdbaths and are drawn to feeders offering peanut butter or a shallow dish of mealworms.

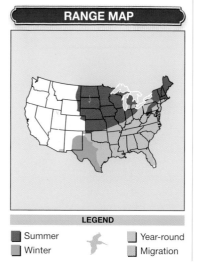

RANGE MAP

LEGEND

■ Summer
■ Winter
■ Year-round
■ Migration

blue

Purple Martin

Southern Native American tribes hung hollow gourds to encourage these useful insectivores to nest nearby, and the tradition continues in the East, where elaborate "hotel" dwellings are constructed to house entire martin colonies. Their pleasing song is a low-pitched rolling twitter.

Description
Recognizable as America's only all-dark swallow, the 7–8 inch bird has pointed wings and a forked tail. Males are glossy purple-black, while females are duller with gray underparts.

Preferred Habitat
Martins make their home in farmland, towns, marshes, deserts, or residential areas. Their populations are declining from competition with house sparrows and starlings.

Feeding Habits
Feeding on the wing, martins consume vast quantities of flying insects, especially dragonflies and airborne spiders.

Migration Habits
In late summer thousands of martins roost together in city shade trees, preparing for their migration to South America. They reach Canada in May, breeding along the Pacific states and the eastern half of the United States.

Placement of Feeders
Martin houses allow an up-close opportunity to observe these colorful birds, but in the West they can also be spotted at ponds or lakes, skimming the water to drink and bathe.

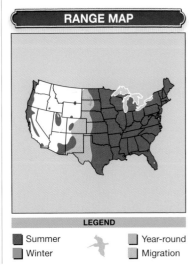

RANGE MAP

LEGEND

■ Summer ■ Year-round
■ Winter ■ Migration

An Old English word for tail is "start" and the male's bright, reddish tail, which he constantly flashes and fans, earns the name. In their Latin American wintering grounds, redstarts are known as *candelita*, or "little flame."

Description

Adult males, at about 5 inches, are glossy black with flame-colored patches on the tail, wings, and sides year-round. Females and young males are pale olive to dark gray above with bright yellow highlights and a white belly.

Preferred Habitat

Redstarts make their home in mixed and deciduous second-growth forests along swamps or streams. The season's brood is raised in a tree-bound nest of moss and grass.

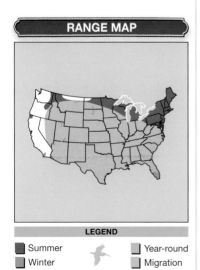

RANGE MAP

LEGEND

- Summer
- Winter
- Year-round
- Migration

Feeding Habits

Restless and active, these small birds are always in motion, scanning foliage for tiny berries, dropping to the ground to munch on seeds, then zooming away to chase an insect with the aid of bristly feathers around the beak.

Migration Habits

Wintering south of the border, the breeding ground for the American redstart consist of most the continental United States.

Placement of Feeders

Watch for a flash of black and orange in the treetops to find these common warblers, who usually respond with interest to birders making a "pishing" or squeaking sound.

black

in bare branches as evidence of their summer residences.

Feeding Habits
Seated in the forest canopy the oriole collects caterpillars, insects, and mulberries, then swoops to ground level to drain nectar from flowers.

Migration Habits
These orioles breed in the East, with the Bullock's covering the West and into Canada. In early September, they migrate south to winter in Mexico and South America.

Placement of Feeders
Before you sight them you will likely hear their clear, whistled *tea-dear-dear-dear* song. The best backyard draws are orange halves, grape jelly, suet, and nectar feeders.

This and the western Bullock's oriole are sometimes classified as the same species, the northern oriole. With the planting of trees across the Great Plains, their ranges overlapped and these distinct-looking birds began to interbreed.

Description
Males are unmistakable, with their black back and head, bright orange belly, black wings barred with white, and orange in the wings and tail. Females have a hint of orange. Juveniles look like females, and the juveniles of both races are nearly identical.

Preferred Habitat
In May the oriole constructs a pendulous pouch nest in the fork of a shade tree to raise its annual brood. In winter look for their beautifully woven nests

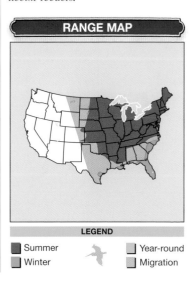

RANGE MAP

LEGEND
- Summer
- Winter
- Year-round
- Migration

Long ago abandoning natural nesting sites for docks, bridges, and barns, this swallow is a common sight in rural and suburban communities. Its forked tail is easily recognizable in flight, and it's the only swallow that flaps continuously, issuing a constant stream of twittering and chattering.

Description

Measuring 5-7 inches long, with a deeply forked tail and pointed wings, the barn swallow is dark blue-black above, with a red throat and pale undersides. Its flight is fast and direct, and may skim close to the ground.

Preferred Habitat

This bird favors open country or marshes near buildings and water, such as golf courses, parks, and farms.

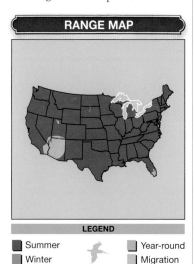

RANGE MAP

LEGEND

- Summer
- Winter
- Year-round
- Migration

It constructs nest made of mud pellets under building eaves or on a beam.

Feeding Habits

They capture insects on the wing, and thus spend more time in flight than almost any other bird. Like other swallows, they skim the surface of rivers or lakes to drink while flying.

Migration Habits

Wintering outside the United States presents no great challenge, as the swallow travels up to 600 miles or more to reach its summer breeding grounds throughout the lower 48 states of the U.S.

Placement of Feeders

Encourage the presence of these helpful insectivores by allowing them to nest in buildings or other man-made structures.

Black Tern

Social and gregarious, these terns usually nest and roost in colonies numbering a few to hundreds of birds.

Feeding Habits

This tern occasionally dives into freshwater for fish and crustaceans, but spends most of its time swooping erratically after flying insects.

Migration Habits

Their summer breeding range stretches from California to New England and north throughout Canada. In autumn they head south and seaward, wintering at sea or along the coasts of Central America, South America, or even far-flung Africa.

Destruction of its marsh habitat has led to drastically reduced populations of these elegant terns. Since its appearance on the Audubon Society's Blue List of threatened species in 1971, efforts continue to preserve and protect its wetland home.

Placement of Feeders

Watch for this carnivore feeding along inland lakes and marshes. Listen for their nasal song or short *kik* call.

Description

This large bird, measuring 9–10.5 inches, is unmistakable in all seasons. Breeding adults are all black, with a grayish tail and white highlights on the wings. Winter birds are gray above, with a black cap, and patchy white below with white side patches.

Preferred Habitat

Alongside freshwater marshes, lagoons, and lakes, black terns build a small hollow nest on floating marsh plants.

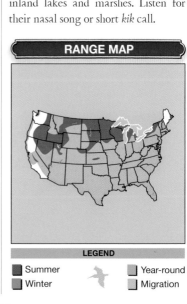

RANGE MAP

LEGEND

- Summer
- Winter
- Year-round
- Migration

black

A thin, 5-inch bird striped black and white all over creeps down a tree trunk. Sometimes nicknamed the black-and-white creeper or nuthatch for its unusual tree-creeping habits, this unmistakable zebra-patterned bird is the oddball of the warbler family.

Description

The male has a black mask and throat in summer, but in winter the throat is white. Females have a white face and throat with a black stripe through the eye. Juveniles are patterned with brown instead of black.

Preferred Habitat

In deciduous and mixed forests of the North and East, these warblers can be found building grass nests concealed with dead leaves on or near the ground at the base of a tree, shrub, rock, or log.

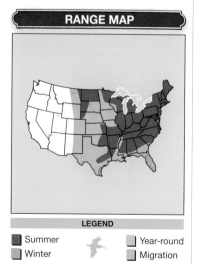

RANGE MAP

LEGEND

■ Summer
□ Winter
■ Year-round
■ Migration

Feeding Habits

Even before the spring leaves unfold, this warbler scours branches and tree trunks upside down, poking into loose bark for insects and larvae, especially spiders and daddy longlegs.

Migration Habits

As early as March flocks appear in the East, heading north to breed throughout Canada. By July the birds are ready to head south, wintering along parts of the Gulf Coast to South America.

Placement of Feeders

Track down their high-pitched, creaky-hinge song of six to eight *wee-see* phrases to observe this cooperative, friendly warbler.

black

Black-capped Chickadee

I n gardens and forests across North America the chickadee's acrobatic antics and sweet *chick-a-dee-dee-dee* call are familiar year-round. The chickadee is friendly and sociable, easily tamed and even hand-fed.

Description
Both sexes measure 5 inches, colored grayish above and pale below, with a bold black cap and bib, white cheeks, and white bars on black wings. In the southwest, the black-capped is replaced by the Carolina chickadee.

Preferred Habitat
Chickadees nest in tree cavities or simple bird boxes in gardens, mixed and deciduous forests, and residential areas.

Feeding Habits
Traveling in small feeding flocks, the birds work together to locate plentiful food sources, particularly in winter. They glean insects and larvae from branches and foliage, as well as seeds and berries.

Migration Habits
Across most of the northern United States from the Great Lakes to the Pacific Northwest chickadees are year-round residents. In autumn they join small mixed flocks of titmice, nuthatches, kinglets, creepers, and warblers to roost and forage together during the harsh winter months.

Placement of Feeders
Seed and suet feeders attract these cheery backyard visitors, and they are usually one of the first birds to find and inhabit a new nesting box.

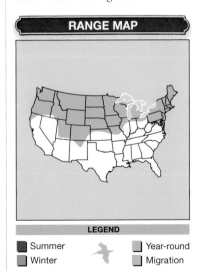

As its name suggests, this heron is most active at night, but can often be seen during daylight feeding along edges of lakes and lagoons or roosting in trees. At sundown, when most herons return to the nest, these birds leave their roosts and set out to hunt.

Description

Hunched and stocky, the night heron measures 22–28 inches. Adults have a black cap and back, red eyes, gray wings, yellow legs, and a white belly. Streaky gray juveniles closely resemble the American bittern.

Preferred Habitat

In marshes, rivers, or wooded swamps, this heron piles up a mass of sticks to craft a messy platform nest. These fragile constructions are often disrupted by

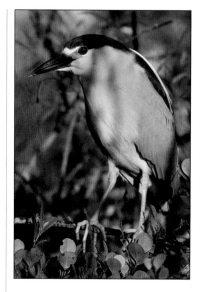

storms or high winds, dumping the chicks unceremoniously on the rubble below the rookery.

Feeding Habits

Silent and menacing, the heron perches on the edge of a pond or marsh waiting for its aquatic prey—frogs, fish, and crustaceans—to chance within range.

Migration Habits

This heron summers throughout almost all states and north into central Canada, and remains year-round along the Pacific, Gulf, and Atlantic Coasts.

Placement of Feeders

Its scientific name, *nycticorax*, means "night raven." Listen for this bird's loud, barking *squawk*, a common nighttime sound.

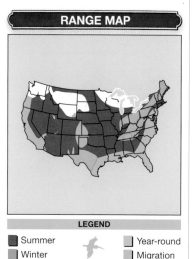

RANGE MAP

LEGEND

- ■ Summer
- ■ Winter
- ■ Year-round
- ■ Migration

black

Blackpoll Warbler

Weighing only half an ounce, the 6-inch blackpoll warbler is America's only small land bird to make the transoceanic journey of 10,000 miles between northern Canada and the rainforests of northeast South America, crossing vast stretches of the Atlantic Ocean and Gulf of Mexico.

Description

Breeding males are streaked black and white, with a black crown and throat and white cheeks. Females, juveniles, and nonbreeding males are greenish with pale legs.

Preferred Habitat

In the spruce forests of Canada's Far North, these hardy birds craft a secure cup of twigs, stems, and grass in a spruce or fir tree, lining the nest with feathers to keep the fledglings warm.

Feeding Habits

Gleaning from foliage or flycatching, the blackpoll consumes caterpillars, spiders, wasps, aphids, mosquitoes, and other insects. In their wintering grounds, the warblers subsist on nectar, fruit, and pollen.

Migration Habits

Crossing thousands of miles each spring and autumn, the blackpoll warbler faces many dangers. They rest and feed by day and migrate at night, often crashing head-on into tall buildings, TV towers, and lighthouses.

Placement of Feeders

The blackpolls are very late migrants through the United States, commonly resting and feeding in oak forests.

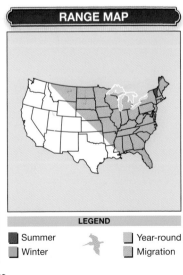

RANGE MAP

LEGEND

■ Summer
■ Winter
■ Year-round
■ Migration

black

Signaling the coming spring with its appearance at California's Capistrano Mission each year, the cliff swallow is known for its elaborate gourd-shaped nests, constructed out of mud on the sides of barns, buildings, or the rocky cliffs for which it is named.

Description

Distinct from the barn swallow for its square tail and pointed wings, this 6-inch swallow is blue-black on top with a white forehead and a rust-colored throat and rump.

Preferred Habitat

Open country with a fresh water source and nearby barns or buildings for nesting is the ideal environment for this bird. Unfortunately, the introduction of the house sparrow, which forces cliff swallows out of nesting

sites, has reduced their population considerably.

Feeding Habits

Like other swallows, these birds snatch flying insects and airborne spiders in flight, and may dip down to drink from the surface of rivers or lakes.

Migration Habits

Widespread in North America in summer, the cliff swallow migrates southward in flocks of hundreds come autumn. They return faithfully to the same nesting sites annually.

Placement of Feeders

Thousands of breeding pairs have been known to nest in a single barn, but be grateful for the innumerable insects they will consume.

RANGE MAP

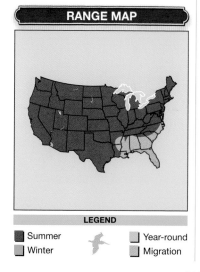

LEGEND

■ Summer   ■ Year-round
□ Winter   ■ Migration

Common Grackle

Feeding Habits

Scanning the ground, scouring trees or shrubs, or wading in water, this black-bird seeks insects, seeds, fruit, grain, salamanders, eggs, or fish, and will consume the young of other birds, reducing its popularity with bird lovers.

Migration Habits

Found year-round in the East and Mid-west, these late migrants congregate by the thousands in late autumn and early spring. Attempts to control their huge flocks have been unsuccessful.

Placement of Feeders

Backyard feeders and public garbage bins alike are subject to raids by these aggressive scavengers. Cracked corn, mixed seeds, suet, and sunflower hearts are sure-fire lures.

I ronically classified as a songbird because it shares with those species a special resonating voice box, the grackle is known for its piercing, high-pitched screech. Its harsh call is reflected in its name, derived from the Latin *graculous* meaning "to cough."

Description

A large bird measuring up to 12.5 inches, the grackle has a long, wedge-shaped tail and yellow eyes. Males appear iridescent bronze or black with purple, greenish, or bronze highlights, while the female is less glossy and shorter tailed.

Preferred Habitat

Grackles are common in groves, towns, farmland, marshes, thickets, or suburban landscapes, where food is plentiful.

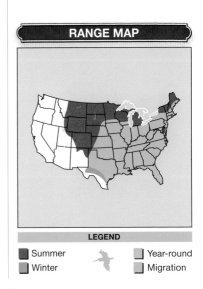

RANGE MAP

LEGEND

■ Summer ■ Year-round
■ Winter ■ Migration

Downy Woodpecker

Downies are the smallest and friendliest of the North American woodpeckers. Like their tree-hammering relatives, a strong bill, neck, and reinforced skull protect the brain from repeated hammering, and bristly feathers protect the nostrils.

Description
This species is a 7-inch version of the hairy woodpecker. The back and belly are white, the black wings spotted white, and the tail barred. Males have a red patch on the head, and both have a thin black mustache.

Preferred Habitat
Any urban or rural area with deciduous trees can be home to this small woodpecker. Mating pairs excavate a cavity in a tree, stump, or fence post to build the nest. Parents share

incubation and feeding duties.

Feeding Habits
Foraging among foliage and under bark with its sharply barbed tongue, the bird consumes insects, larvae, and grubs. In winter they can be found in weedy fields, consuming dormant wasps and corn-borers.

Migration Habits
The downy is found in almost all of North America, remaining in the North all winter to forage with chickadees and kinglets in Mid-Atlantic backyards.

Placement of Feeders
Feeding stations featuring berries, beef suet, peanut butter, pecans, or sunflower seeds will be home to plucky downies, especially in winter.

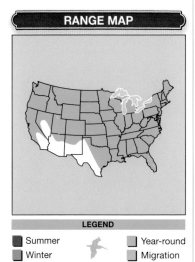

RANGE MAP

LEGEND

■ Summer
■ Winter
■ Year-round
■ Migration

Eastern Phoebe

From its perch on a dead branch, an unremarkable 7-inch bird sweetly chants *fee-bee* over and over. Suddenly a flying insect catches its eye, and it darts out to snatch it, returning swiftly to its favorite perch.

Description
This phoebe is best distinguished from other flycatchers by its lack of wing bars or eye ring. It is gray-brown or olive above and white below, with a black bill.

Preferred Habitat
Phoebes prefer to live near a freshwater source but are well adapted to living among human developments. They attach mud nests to vertical walls, barn rafters, windowsills, and bridge supports. Hard-working females raise two broods each season.

Feeding Habits
For most of the year its diet consists entirely of flying insects, but in winter it subsists on the fruit and berries of poison ivy and poison sumac, and may even scoop little fish from shallow water.

Migration Habits
This hardy flycatcher has a long breeding season in the East and central Canada, with most wintering in the Southeast and in Mexico.

Placement of Feeders
Although tame and common in suburbs and farmland, the eastern phoebe rarely visits feeding stations. The best field mark is the constant downward "wagging" of its long tail.

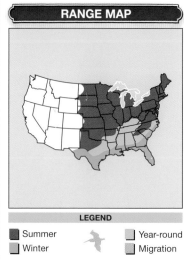

RANGE MAP

LEGEND

- ■ Summer
- □ Winter
- □ Year-round
- ▨ Migration

In 1890 a Shakespeare enthusiast released 100 starlings in New York City in an effort to introduce all feathered friends mentioned in Shakespeare's works. Now numbering 200 million, starlings are noisy and messy, but they consume a large quantity of insects.

Description

Shiny black with a green or purple sheen in summer, the bird molts in autumn, growing a winter coat of white-speckled feathers. The stout, 7.5-inch starling is a skillful imitator known for its wolf-whistle call.

Preferred Habitat

Especially common around landfills or grain elevators, the starling is at home in cities, suburbs, or farmland. The female constructs a nest of twigs and trash in a tree or cavity.

Feeding Habits

City dwellers and rural residents alike can spot these birds probing for insects, spiders, worms, fruit, grain, or seeds from parks to farmyards.

Migration Habits

This native of Eurasia is found year-round from central Canada to northern Mexico. During colder months they fly in enormous swarms to roost in warmer downtown areas.

Placement of Feeders

Starlings are drawn to seed and suet feeders, but if you intend your nest boxes for native species such as bluebirds, woodpeckers, or purple martins, monitor them carefully for starling habitation.

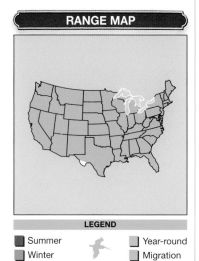

RANGE MAP

LEGEND

■ Summer
■ Winter
■ Year-round
■ Migration

black

Hairy Woodpecker

Woodpeckers are not known for vocalization, and despite their sharp *peek* call, the birds prefer to regale each other with a drumming "song" made by jackhammering dead tree trunks with their stout bills.

Description
Larger than the similar downy woodpecker, the 9-inch hairy species is mainly black above, with white-spotted wings and a white back, and white below. The head has a black crown, stripes on the face, and small red patches. Juveniles are brown.

Preferred Habitat
This shy forest bird is found in mixed and coniferous forests, wooded swamps, and river bottoms. In the spring parent birds busily excavate a cavity in a tree or shrub to house their eggs.

Feeding Habits
Using its sturdy tail like a tripod, this woodpecker hammers into tree trunks and shreds strips of bark to excavate wood-boring insects, bark beetles, ants, and spiders, or the occasional hazelnut or acorn.

Migration Habits
Regardless of the season or weather conditions, this bird can be found in all states, cheerily chipping away loose tree bark.

Placement of Feeders
The hairy woodpecker is not so common a backyard visitor as the downy, but it is drawn to raw apples, bananas, peanut butter, and sunflower seeds, and it is especially fond of beef suet.

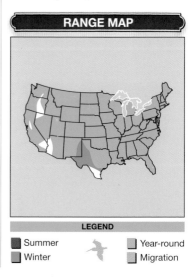

RANGE MAP

LEGEND

Summer
Winter
Year-round
Migration

The first flycatcher ever classified by American ornithologists was found in Acadia, an old name for Nova Scotia. Later, several of these similar-looking species were distinguished and renamed. This bird retains the original moniker, despite the fact that its northernmost range lies in Connecticut.

Description
Adults measure 6.5 inches long, with olive grayish-green plumage above, a white throat and yellow belly, two pale wing bars, and a bold yellow eye ring. The greenish juvenile has a scaly appearance.

Preferred Habitat
Mature, deciduous forests or bottomland swamps are the best locales to seek the Acadian. In a maple or beech tree, the female builds a loose nest high above the ground, often over water or paved roads.

Feeding Habits
This insectivore hovers above branches or leaves seeking spiders, bees, wasps, ants, and insect larvae. Small fruit and berries supplement their diet in winter.

Migration Habits
In North America the Acadian flycatcher is a summer visitor, appearing in late April for breeding from eastern Texas northward and east to the coast.

Placement of Feeders
These common migrants are active and aggressive, giving a stunning aerial courtship chase with a sharp *ti-ti-ti-ti* call. Also listen for their unique *peet-sa* call.

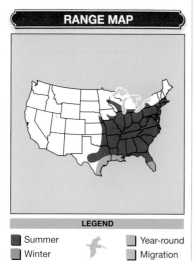

RANGE MAP

LEGEND

- Summer
- Winter
- Year-round
- Migration

gray

American Pipit

Tiny but hardy, the pipit nests only in the harsh tundra environment. American birders are likely to see them during migration, where they rest in mud flats and wet grain fields, though nesting pairs do appear throughout the Rocky Mountain range.

Description
Breeding birds, at 5–7 inches long, are grayish above and buff below with a white-rimmed tail. Autumn birds are streaky gray-brown above and heavily streaked white below. The thin legs and beak are dark.

Preferred Habitat
Males establish nesting territories on alpine or Arctic tundra before the snow melts, ready for a quick breeding season. During nonbreeding season they can be found on dunes, plowed fields, and shores.

Feeding Habits
Walking slowly on sturdy legs, the pipit consumes insects, spiders, snails, mayflies, and dragonflies and their larvae. In winter it eats mainly seeds.

Migration Habits
In March males head to their breeding range in the Rocky Mountains north to Alaska and the Arctic Circle, while females follow in May. In September, flocks head south to the southern United States and Central and South America.

Placement of Feeders
The pipit seldom stops to perch, but listen for its quick *pipit* call in flight and observe its constant tail-bobbing action.

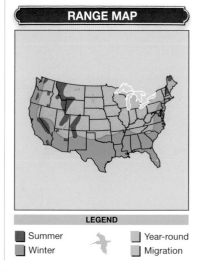

RANGE MAP

LEGEND

Summer Year-round
Winter Migration

As the herald of spring in northern states, the robin's chipper call of *cheerily cheer up cheerio* pierces the early morning stillness. Although technically a thrush—and the only widespread thrush in America—the bird is named for its resemblance to the red-breasted robin of Europe.

Description

The male, at 9–11 inches long, is gray on top, with a black head and bright red breast. The female is similar in appearance but duller, with a gray head.

Preferred Habitat

Lawns, gardens, parks, forests, and farmland are favorite locations, but birds that winter in the northern states may roost in cedar bogs and swamps.

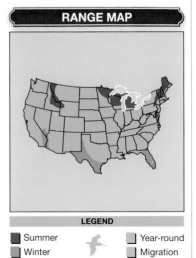

RANGE MAP

LEGEND

■ Summer ■ Year-round
■ Winter ■ Migration

Feeding Habits

As it hops across a lawn with its head cocked, the robin is hunting for insects and earthworms. Berries provide sustenance through the winter.

Migration Habits

Though not all robins head south for the winter, each year huge flocks of up to 300,000 birds head northward in spring, with each bird returning to the area of his birth.

Placement of Feeders

While not regular visitors to feeders, they may be drawn to mealworms, bread, raisins, or fruit. They are easily sighted on a grassy lawn rooting for worms, and may build nests on ledges or windowsills.

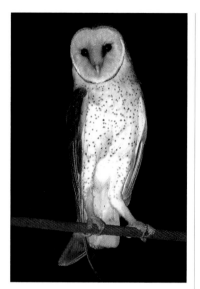

Feeding Habits

Garbage dumps, cemeteries, and farms are favorite hunting grounds for rodents, small mammals, or other birds. The owl has good daytime eyesight, but can track its prey by sound alone in complete darkness.

Migration Habits

The barn owl inhabits almost all states year-round, laying eggs in buildings, hollow trees, caves, or burrows. They also practice population control, producing few or no eggs when food is scarce.

Placement of Feeders

These nocturnal hunters can be seen soaring alongside highways or rural roads at dusk as they scan the ground for prey, and they may select a local barn or bell tower for nesting.

Piercing the night with a spine-tingling hiss and scream, the barn owl pursues an evening meal of mice or rabbits. This owl species is tolerant of human presence, often making its home in barns.

Description

The barn owl, at 13–19 inches long, is easily recognized by its long legs, dark eyes, and heart-shaped face. Colored golden brown with a greyish hue above and white below, it appears pure white in flight.

Preferred Habitat

A widespread species, the barn owl is found on six of seven continents, where it inhabits grasslands, marshes, deserts, and residential and urban areas.

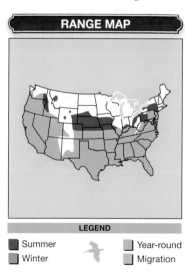

RANGE MAP

LEGEND

■ Summer   ■ Year-round
□ Winter   □ Migration

Along a quiet river bank, a large blue-gray bird with a ragged crest issues a rattling *crick-crick-crick* from a nearby perch. The kingfisher is an aggressive, independent hunter.

Description

Pigeon-sized at 11–14 inches long, this crested bird is blue-gray above with a crest and white collar. The male has a blue-gray band across the chest, while the female has two chest bands and brighter coloring.

Preferred Habitat

These fish-eaters never stray far from water. The mating pair tunnels into the bank alongside a favorite river or lake, where the female lays eggs in the cool, dark burrow.

RANGE MAP

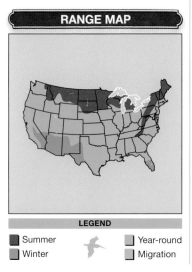

LEGEND

- ■ Summer
- ■ Winter
- ■ Year-round
- ■ Migration

Feeding Habits

Hovering over the water, a flash of blue spirals into a deadly dive, clutching a stunned fish back to its perch, where it beats the fish and swallows it whole. Bones and scales are later regurgitated as pellets. Favorite foods include fish, tadpoles, salamanders, frogs, insects, crabs, or crayfish. Young are taught to retrieve dead fish from the water.

Migration Habits

Found year-round throughout most of the west, this fierce fisher travels to northern border states during summer only.

Placement of Feeders

Patient observation along the water's edge will reveal favorite perches and may allow you to witness their diving spectacle.

gray

Carolina Chickadee

This perky species is very similar to the black-capped chickadee, but their ranges replace each other geographically. Its four-syllable *phee-bee, phee-bay* whistle is twice as long as the black-cap's song.

Description
At only 4.5 inches the Carolina chickadee is one of smallest in its family. The handsome bird is gray above and pale buff below, with a black cap and bib, and white cheeks.

Preferred Habitat
These chickadees are woodland birds, residing in deciduous, mixed, and coniferous forest, wooded swamps, gardens, and parks. In a tree cavity or birdhouse the chickadee crafts a cup-shaped nest of moss, plants, and feathers.

Feeding Habits
Insects, especially agricultural pests, make up about half of the chickadee's diet, supplemented by berries and seeds from shrubs, pines, and weeds. Usually traveling in pairs or small groups, chickadees swiftly communicate each flock member's successful foraging location or strategy.

Migration Habits
In the Southeast these birds are a common permanent resident from Texas to New Jersey. In autumn, they join up with mixed flocks of kinglets, creepers, warblers, titmice, and nuthatches.

Placement of Feeders
Backyards with sufficient trees and shrubbery are often host to the cheery chickadee, who readily visits seed feeders with its mixed flock.

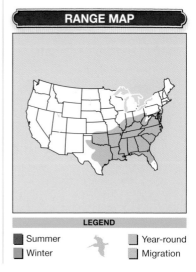

RANGE MAP

LEGEND

Summer

Winter

Year-round

Migration

gray

This Arctic finch of northern Canada survives colder temperatures more than any other songbird. Sociable and nonterritorial even in nesting season, redpolls travel in flocks that irregularly visit the northern states during winter.

Description
The best field marks of the 5-inch redpoll are its raspberry-red cap and black chin. Adults are streaky gray-brown above with a white belly, and males have red on the chest and rump.

Preferred Habitat
Breeding in Arctic tundra, birch groves, and northern coniferous forest, the female builds a small, heavily insulated nest on a platform of twigs. In winter flocks are found in brushy or weedy fields and thickets.

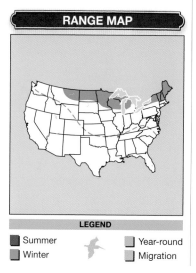

RANGE MAP

LEGEND
- Summer
- Winter
- Year-round
- Migration

Feeding Habits
To meet its energy needs the bird eats constantly, foraging on the ground for seeds of pine, hemlock, birch, and alder, various grass seeds, and buds of trees and shrubs. The bird also has a special pouch in its esophagus for delayed digesting.

Migration Habits
Generally redpolls live year-round in Canada, but in harsh winters large flocks wander southward in search of warmer climates. Some have been spotted as far south as Nebraska and as far west as Washington.

Placement of Feeders
In mixed flocks of goldfinches and siskins, the tame redpoll readily visits backyard feeders for niger and sunflower seeds.

gray

Cooper's Hawk

Once known as the "chicken hawk" for its preference for barnyard fowl, this large hawk was hunted by the thousands, and many other hawk species suffered the same fate. Populations also diminished temporarily with the use of DDT.

Description
This species is almost identical to the sharp-shinned hawk, but larger and more powerful at 15–20 inches long. Adults are dark blue-gray above and white-barred red below, with a dark cap. Juveniles are streaked with brown.

Preferred Habitat
Open deciduous forests and mixed woodlands are traditional habitats of Cooper's hawks, but they are increasingly common in urban and suburban yards. In their high platform nest of sticks, the male feeds the incubating female, and she feeds the chicks.

Feeding Habits
The large hawk is easily outmaneuvered by songbirds, but it relies on surprise and speed to catch birds, squirrels, and chipmunks. It may return with its captured meal to a feeding roost.

Migration Habits
The species is found year-round in almost all states except the Great Plains, breeding slightly north into southern Canada and wintering in the lower majority of its range.

Placement of Feeders
These woodland birds are best identified as they glide overhead by their rounded wings and long, rounded tail.

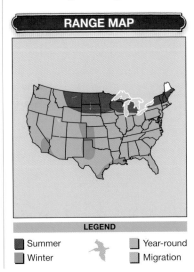

RANGE MAP

LEGEND

■ Summer	■ Year-round
■ Winter	■ Migration

Dark-eyed Junco

The dark-eyed species consolidates what were formerly thought to be up to five different species: the slate-colored, Oregon, white-winged, pink-sided, and gray-headed juncos. But despite their varied coloring, these birds breed freely with each other, and all issue a similar, slow, musical trill.

Description

All measuring 5–6.5 inches long, with a pinkish bill and dark eyes, there are distinct plumage variations. The eastern slate bird is gray above and below; the gray-head of the southern Rockies is rust or brown above; the pink-sided junco of the Central Rockies has pinkish marks on its sides; the Oregon variety has a black head and brown back, while the white-winged version of the Black Hills has white wing bars and tail.

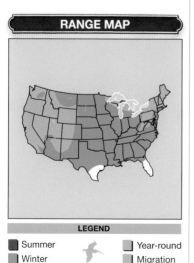

RANGE MAP

LEGEND
- Summer
- Winter
- Year-round
- Migration

Preferred Habitat

Juncos live in open woodlands and clearings throughout North America.

Feeding Habits

With a unique double-scratching motion, juncos dig for insects. They also enjoy seeds and berries.

Migration Habits

Found throughout the continental United States in the winter and migrating north in summer, the junco nests on the ground and maintains a rigid flock hierarchy. It can be found year-round throughout the western third of the United States.

Placement of Feeders

This frequent feeder visitor prefers millet, sunflower hearts, and finely cracked corn from low platform feeders.

gray

Eastern Screech Owl

Two distinct colorings define this small owl—rusty red or mottled gray-brown. Unaffected by season, sex, or age, each bird's permanent coloring varies by relative population in a given habitat.

Description

Identified by its distinctive ear tufts, fixed yellow eyes, and white wing spots, the 10-inch red or gray owl gives a variety of chilling calls, including screeching, purring, trilling, and a descending wail.

Preferred Habitat

The eastern species prefers mature deciduous forest, lakeshores, orchards, or open forest, as well as suburban areas. The female lays eggs in a tree—especially small red cedars—or nest box.

Feeding Habits

Hunting at night on silent wings, the owl scoops up rodents, birds, earthworms, and snakes with its deadly talons. It can also catch insects on the wing or plunge into streams to snatch fish.

Migration Habits

The eastern screech owl is a year-round resident east of the Rockies, but on rare occasion has been spotted as far west as the mountains of Montana.

Placement of Feeders

Birders may never detect the owl's nighttime visits to backyard birdbaths, but the elusive guest sometimes uses nest boxes. Listen for their loud horse-whinny calls after dark.

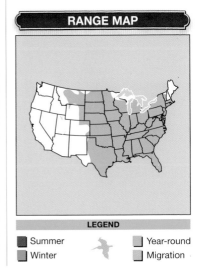

RANGE MAP

LEGEND

Summer
Winter
Year-round
Migration

Small and nondescript, this bird carols a sweet *pee-o-wee* whistle, one of the best-loved bird songs. But during nesting season the usually gentle creature doesn't hesitate to chase off gray squirrels, grackles, robins, and jays.

Description

Like the eastern phoebe, this bird is gray above and white below, but with two white wing bars. The 6.5-inch adult is identical to the western wood pewee, but these two species have very distinct songs.

Preferred Habitat

Wood pewees are found in mature woodlands, orchards, parks, and groves. In a deciduous tree, the female constructs a strong, shallow nest out of moss and plant fibers coated with lichens, disguised as a knot on the limb.

Feeding Habits

From its watchful perch, the wood pewee darts out to snatch a flying insect, a technique known as "hawking." Its favorite foods include flies, gnats, and other small insects, and wild berries in winter.

Migration Habits

In early May small flocks travel from their Central and South American wintering grounds to favorite breeding sites across the East.

Placement of Feeders

On summer days this feathered friend sings all day long from a high perch. But don't be fooled by the European starling's skillful imitation of the bird's plaintive song.

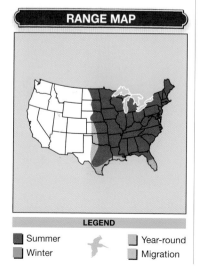

RANGE MAP

LEGEND

☐ Summer   ☐ Year-round
☐ Winter   ☐ Migration

gray

Gray Catbird

Feeding Habits

Ants, beetles, moths, grasshoppers, dragonflies, and spiders are found by foraging on the ground and in shrubs, while berries of the dogwood, mulberry, elderberry, and wild grape trees round out the catbird's diet.

Migration Habits

In summer, the catbird breeds across most of the continent, while it winters in the Carolinas and southward. These nighttime migrators often collide with aerial antennae and TV towers.

Placement of Feeders

This boisterous garden visitor may take up residence in a tangle of shrubs or briars alongside a house and is fond of birdbaths.

Second only to the mockingbird for its impressive mimicry, the male catbird, with a special ability to sing two notes at once, fills the air with a medley of area birdcalls, shrieks, whistles, and its notorious cat-like whine.

Description

Long and thin, the catbird measures 8–9.75 inches, colored dark gray above with a black cap, and a dark rust patch on its rump.

Preferred Habitat

The catbird is at home in thickets, brush, and gardens, where it raises two broods each season in a tangle of vines or shrubs. Though tolerant of certain species, the gray catbird is territorial and may pierce the eggs of other songbirds, including cowbird eggs found in its own nest.

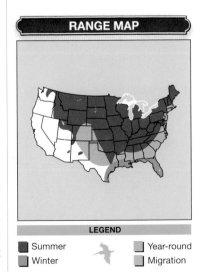

RANGE MAP

LEGEND

Summer | Year-round
Winter | Migration

gray

From dawn to dusk and sometimes all through the night, the northern mockingbird croons a steady, rapid stream of hundreds of bird songs, interspersed with occasional barking dog and chirping cricket imitations. Its Latin name means "mimic of many tongues."

Description

This slender, gray bird measures 9–11 inches, with a long black tail bordered by white that it flicks from side to side. Both sexes flash their two white wing bars and large white side patches.

Preferred Habitat

Fiercely territorial, mockingbirds will attack crows and grackles, and even cats during breeding season. They will also attack their own reflections with enough violence to cause injury or occasionally death. In lawns, gardens, farmland, or deserts, they live on the ground, hiding in bushes as needed, but mounting a high perch to sing.

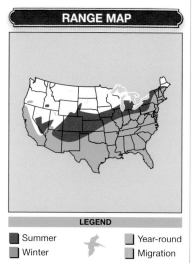

RANGE MAP

LEGEND

■ Summer
■ Winter
■ Year-round
■ Migration

Feeding Habits

This ground feeder forages in foliage and short grass for insects, grasshoppers, spiders, and fruit.

Migration Habits

Found year-round from California to Texas to the Mid-Atlantic, mockingbirds may migrate north in summer.

Placement of Feeders

Mockingbirds are heard singing at night more than other birds in their family, and can be identified in flight by their white wing patches and extremely slow wing beats. Suet and raisins are favorites at the feeder.

gray

Tufted Titmouse

B reeding season makes titmice anxious and irritable, and they are notorious for pulling hair from sleeping dogs, cats, and livestock to line their nests. But their cheery, ringing *peter, peter, peter!* charms at the winter feeder.

Description
Sparrow-sized at 6.5 inches, the crested bird is gray above, whitish below, with buff flanks and rusty sides. Those in Texas and Oklahoma have a black crest.

Preferred Habitat
Mating pairs seek bottomlands and wet forests, raising their brood in a hole in a mature oak tree. In autumn they roam deciduous forests with a mixed flock, frequenting gardens and parks.

Feeding Habits
Clinging to a branch, the titmouse swings upside down to pluck spiders and insects from the underside of foliage. Acorn masts and oak galls are favorites in autumn, as well as fruit and seeds.

Migration Habits
For most of the year these birds travel in pairs, but in autumn they join with small flocks of chickadees, kinglets, and nuthatches for social foraging. From Nebraska eastward they are common year-round.

Placement of Feeders
Beechnuts, acorns, and shelled peanuts score big with these noisy, friendly backyard visitors, and mating pairs that select a nesting box on your property will stay all year.

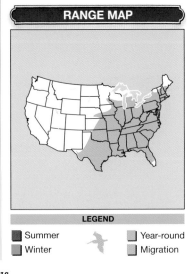

RANGE MAP

LEGEND

■ Summer   ■ Year-round
■ Winter   ■ Migration

An extra long hind toe claw allows the nuthatch to creep down tree trunks headfirst. Like its red-breasted relative, the white-breasted nuthatch gives a low-pitched *yank-yank* call and a low whistled song, including a *whi-whi-whi-whi* mating song.

Description

Larger than the red-breast, this bird measures 5–6 inches, colored blue-gray above with a black crown and white underparts. Its black eye is conspicuous in a white face.

Preferred Habitat

Mating pairs remain together year-round, usually in dry oak or pine oak forests or other deciduous forests. Adult birds nest in a natural cavity or bird box, or excavate a new hole.

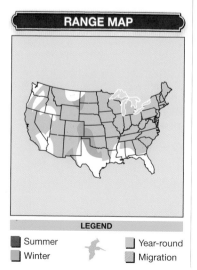

RANGE MAP

LEGEND

- Summer
- Winter
- Year-round
- Migration

Feeding Habits

Using its long, thin bill, the nuthatch forages under loose bark and in tree crevices for insects and larvae.

Migration Habits

Nuthatches are found year-round in almost all continental states. Occasionally they migrate to the outer coasts in winter but are usually sedentary. In winter nuthatches join flocks of chickadees, woodpeckers, and kinglets to roam for food within their territories.

Placement of Feeders

Seed feeders and suet cakes draw these familiar winter visitors to backyard feeders. They are cheery and friendly, though not tame, and will use available nest boxes.

white

White-throated Sparrow

A mong white-throated sparrows, two coloring variations occur—white head stripes or tan head stripes—and birds tend to choose mating pairs with the opposite coloring. Their clear, whistled song has been transcribed in several ways, but *sweet, sweet Canada, Canada, Canada* is a common translation.

Description

The sexes look the same, measuring 6–7 inches long, streaked brown above and buff or gray below. Both have a conspicuous white throat patch, a dark bill, and yellow patches between the eyes.

Preferred Habitat

Brushy undergrowth in coniferous forests is the sparrow's preferred breeding ground, where it builds a nest of grass and moss on or near the ground under small trees. In winter, they are found in brushy areas, pastures, bogs, and suburbs.

Feeding Habits

The sparrow captures insects by scratching on the ground, scouring vegetation, or flycatching. Weed seeds and the fruit of dogwood, sumac, and elderberry trees are also favorites.

Migration Habits

Best known in the United States as a winter visitor, they reside across most of the East and along the West Coast, with a breeding range in the North.

Placement of Feeders

In cold months, backyard bushes may be filled with roosting white-throats. They are drawn to feeders offering cracked corn or seeds.

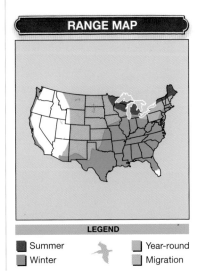

RANGE MAP

LEGEND

■ Summer ■ Year-round
■ Winter ■ Migration

white

INDEX

INDEX